Perry, Lloyd Merle.
Biblical sermon guide

D1776443

Biblical Sermon Guide

Biblical Sermon Guide

A STEP-BY-STEP PROCEDURE

for the

PREPARATION AND PRESENTATION

by

LLOYD M. PERRY

BAKER BOOK HOUSE • GRAND RAPIDS, MICHIGAN 49506

Copyright © 1970 by
Baker Book House Company

Library of Congress Card Catalog Number 75-115642
Printed in the United States of America

ISBN: 0-8010-6856-8

Second printing, July 1973

PREFACE

Preachers may be born preachers, but they are not born ready-made! Preaching is an art, a science, and a labor which, to be successful, must be a labor of love.

The message of the Biblical preacher is the most important message in the world. It calls for an all-out human effort coupled with the supernatural moving of the Holy Spirit, in both preparation and presentation. This involves hard work. There is no substitute. An audience may be inspired and informed by the preacher whose organization of material and ease of delivery is apparent, but they will be wholly unaware of the hours of just plain hard work that has entered into the preparation preceding the presentation. As one grows in experience, he develops some study methods of his own and must learn to tailor his presentation to his own personality — but how does he get started?

This book is a primer. It is not a book for lazy preachers. Nor is it for those who have abandoned the Bible as a basis and source of preaching. The emphasis throughout is on the use of the Scriptures in both the preparation and the presentation of the message. It is a book for those who want to labor in the Gospel and it is geared primarily to those who wish to excel in Biblical preaching but whose opportunities to learn the preparation process have been limited.

This book is based on actual classroom experience, since the author has, for many years, taught practical theology on the seminary level. It is also based on pastoral experience since much of his practical knowledge has been acquired as a pastor. The author is himself an outstanding pulpiteer.

But is is much more than a work on the preparation and presentation of a Biblical sermon. It is rich in suggestions of texts and topics and contains one of the finest bibliographies on preaching that this writer has ever seen. The author's section on adjusting to the type of audience — Apathetic, Believing, Doubtful, and Hostile — is unique and of great practical value, for it is not only the message, the medium, and the messenger which must be considered. After all, the target of preaching is the heart and will of the listener.

Today's empty pews may be in part attributed to the mediocre preaching from many pulpits. But a skilled craftsman in the pulpit still attracts an audience, gains the ear, and moves the heart of the listener. This is not only the result of divine inspiration but is by human design.

ARNOLD T. OLSON

CONTENTS

Preface 5
Introduction 9
Preparing to Preach 11

I. **Preparation of Material for the Biblical Sermon** 13
   A. General Preparation 15
   B. Selecting a Preaching Portion 17
   C. Studying a Preaching Portion 19

II. **Organization of the Outline for the Biblical Sermon** 25
   A. The Sermonic Process of Modification 27
      The Eight Steps of the Modification Process 29
      The Logical Relationship of the Parts of a Sermon Outline 39
      The Scriptural Foundation of the Parts of a Sermon .. 40
   B. The Sermonic Process of Clarification 42
      By Developing an Analogy or Comparison 43
      By Providing Definitions for a Significant English Bible Word 44
      By Giving Applications of a Doctrinal Truth 45
      By Giving Illustrations of a Principle 46
      By Drawing Inferences from Words and Phrases ... 48
      By Showing the Development of a Spiritual Truth ... 49
      By Identifying Individuals or Groups 50
   C. The Sermonic Process of Investigation 51
   D. The General Process of Sermon Outline Organization .. 55

III. **Variation of the Outline for the Biblical Sermon** 61
   A. By Using a Different Sermon Structure 63
   B. By Using Different Biblical Subject Matter 67
   C. By Using Different-Sized Portions of the Bible 79
   D. By Using a Starting Sermon Idea from an Extra-Biblical Source 80
   E. By Placing Special Emphasis Upon the Purpose of the Sermon 85
   F. By Varying the Items within the Sermon Outline Proposition 90
      Conclusion 92
      Illustrations 93

IV. **Presentation of the Biblical Sermon** 95
   A. Plan Your Preaching for the Special Days and Seasons ... 97
      1. Consider the Chronological Relationship 100

    2. Consider the Special Emphases of the Months of
       the Year 101
    3. Consider the Special Days........................102
    4. Consider the Special Occasions...................107
B. Employ Different Methods of Presentation............111
C. Adjust the Type of Presentation to the Type of
    Audience 113
    1. The Apathetic Audience 114
    2. The Believing Audience 115
    3. The Doubtful Audience 116
    4. The Hostile Audience 118
D. Incorporate Dialogue in the Presentation.............120

Bibliography 123

INTRODUCTION

This book presents in practical useable form a step-by-step process for the preparation and presentation of Biblical sermons. The guide aims at practicality and not verbosity. The sermonizer can place it upon his study desk during each process of sermonizing. It is compact enough to be convenient and organized in such a way as to make the material accessible.

The preparation of material for the Biblical sermon involves the discovery of subject matter for the sermon. This was known as *invention* in Classical Rhetoric. The book entitled *How to Search the Scriptures* by Perry and Culver, Baker Book House, will provide helpful methods for studying the Scriptures from the point of view of sermonizing.

The three sermonic processes of *modification, clarification,* and *investigation* are basic sermonic processes for the preacher. He should master these and then proceed to vary them in accord with the material, occasion or his own personal idiosyncrasies. There is no attempt made to put all preachers into one sermon mold. There is an attempt, however, to provide him with a methodology which will deliver him from homiletical frustration.

Variety is a necessary ingredient of effective preaching. We do not strive for variety for its own sake but rather to enhance communication. This guide suggests possibilities for change in *structure, subject matter, sources, purposes,* and *sermon outline items.* The sermon ideas and source books will provide a mine of material for exploration. The basic nature of the message of the sermon should not change but its method of presentation should.

It is expedient for the preacher to plan ahead. He will start his Sunday sermons on Tuesday, prepare his midweek message on Wednesday and complete his Sunday morning message on Friday, his Sunday evening message on Saturday. He will want to plan in terms of the yearly calendar. This demands that he recognize special days and seasons as well as special emphases for individual months. He may find it helpful to have folders available for sermons in process.

The guide suggests that the sermon should be formulated in terms of the congregation to which it is to be presented. We should preach to people. The presentation will, therefore, be varied in terms of the four types of audiences: *apathetic, believing, doubtful,* and *hostile.* The average church congregation often has some of each type within it. We as preachers should respect the ideas of the listeners. It will prove profitable to explore methods of incorporating dialogue within the traditional preaching situation.

PREPARING TO PREACH

A MAN IN CONTACT WITH GOD

SEEKING

The Guidance of the Holy Spirit

To Refresh *To Reveal* *To Restrain*

A MAN IN CONTACT WITH PEOPLE

SERVING

in

Visitation Evangelism Edification

A MAN IN CONTACT WITH SCRIPTURE

SEARCHING

66 Books 31,176 Verses
1,189 Chapters 2,930 Bible Personalities

SELECTING A PREACHING PORTION

Consider:
God's Will — The Needs of the People — The Preacher's Development

Content
of the
Preaching Portion

STUDYING

Context
of the
Preaching Portion

I

PREPARATION OF MATERIAL FOR THE BIBLICAL SERMON

I. PREPARATION OF MATERIAL FOR THE BIBLICAL SERMON

A. General Preparation

The origination or discovery of ideas or concepts for a sermon involves both general and specific preparation on the part of the preacher. General preparation involves his systematic and general cultural development whereas specific preparation consists in securing a mental mastery of the specific subject to be used in a planned address.

The preacher should make himself increasingly familiar with the great subjects that belong to religion and its expression. Some of the general sources to which the speaker may go for material include observation, reading, and conversation. He will want to read in the classics, biography, philosophy, history, poetry, and fiction. There will be a need for his establishing a firm grounding in all aspects of theology. He will want to study contemporary life by observing trends and by observing individuals. Newspapers and periodicals will be of great assistance. He should read great printed sermons and the printed orations of effective speakers. Above all else, he must be a student of Scripture. The open secret of the success of many preachers is that they put their strength and time into collecting suitable materials for discourse.

Independent observation, reflection, conversation, and travel in his own and other lands provides growth and maturity. Personal participation or sympathetic sharing in the experiences of life and death, sins and sorrow, struggles and defeats, triumphs and glories will provide an understanding of life in today's world.

From the beginning of his ministry, the preacher should have definite morning study hours. No less than four hours a day for five days a week should be set aside for this preparation. Certain hours will be set aside for Bible study and certain hours for collateral reading in theology, history, philosophy, etc. A period of time should be devoted to personal spiritual upbuilding through prayer and Bible reading. One famous preacher gained poise and power in the pulpit by spending an hour in his study for every hundred words which he wrote in his sermon.

Homiletics books have offered the following additional suggestions for enhancing one's general preparation for preaching.

    Think while walking.

    Keep a notebook for ideas.

    Systematize one's use of time.

Spread the preparation for a sermon over days, not hours.
Make use of the Biblical languages.
Mark the books read in order that you may locate the material later.
Give thoughtful consideration to the acquisition of books.
Pay attention to the needs of people.
Sermonize when the mind is clear.
Take notes while reading.
Emphasize the study of truth rather than error.
Read the following:
  The Improvement of the Mind by Isaac Watts
  Decision of Character by John Foster
  The Yale Lectures by Henry Ward Beecher

John Bright read the poets for the enrichment of his preaching style. H. P. Liddon read a sermon a day for years and mastered the thought and method of such great preachers as Bossuet, Massillon, and Schleiermacher. Phillips Brooks studied the sermons of Robertson, Bushnell, Martineau, Maurice, and others. J. H. Jowett gave careful study to all of his great English-speaking contemporaries in order to correct his own tendency of giving a one-sided treatment to his themes.

Some preachers of the past have indicated chronological steps taken by them in the process of specific preparation for sermonizing. Charles Kingsley chose his subject for the sermon on the preceding Sunday evening, rested on Monday and sketched a sermon outline on Tuesday. This was then put aside for two days and then finished on Friday. Phillips Brooks chose his theme on Monday and collected material until Wednesday at which time he began to write. His sermon would be completed by Friday. J. H. Jowett began his preparation on Tuesday and spent two days thinking and writing. Not until the central idea of his sermon could be crystalized into one short sentence was a theme ready for serious work in his study.

Edgar DeWitt Jones began his sermon preparation on Monday. He selected the subject and then drew up a rough draft of six to seven hundred words. The material was then dictated directly to his secretary while he paced the floor. This manuscript would consist of about fifteen hundred words. He would then take it home with him and improve it. By Friday, the final copy would be complete. Saturday was kept free. On Sunday morning, he rose at an early hour and went over the service and the sermon.

The logical order of sermon preparation is first to gather the materials of which it is to be composed, then to select what is most fitting and arrange the whole into perfect order. The plan or outline of the sermon should be formulated before attempting to write out the sermon. Writing as a means of sermon preparation, like preaching itself, should be done in a spirit of prayer and conducted under the influence and aid of the Holy Spirit. In the initial writing, the preacher should write as much as possible at a single sitting. If composition slows down, he is advised to stop and read what he has already written. He may then leave it for awhile and return to it a bit later.

In writing a sermon, the preacher should make careful revision of that which he has written. Though he does not write the entire sermon, some part of each sermon should be written. Writing develops self-discipline and stimulates thinking. It increases vocabulary and secures for the preacher the means of profiting by his past labors. Even if the preacher never uses his manuscript in the pulpit, the greater condensation, clarity, and picturesqueness gained through writing will prove profitable. Some have suggested that at least one sermon a week be written in order that the preacher may gain the benefits noted earlier in the paragraph.

The general preparation for preaching should equip the sermonizer to give careful consideration to the selection of a preaching portion. He must be able to sense the will of God. This involves a knowledge of the Word of God, a sensitivity to the witness of the Holy Spirit, and a realistic evaluation of the works of providence. The depths of his own cultural, mental, sociological, and spiritual development influences his selection of a Scripture portion for preaching. The sermonizer must know his strength and limitations. General preparation for preaching will also help him know the needs of the people to whom he is preaching.

B. Selecting a Preaching Portion

The process of specific sermon preparation involves the crystalizing of a "sermon starter." This is an area, passage, need, or idea which is laid upon the heart and mind of the sermonizer as being a possible foundation for a specific sermon. This sermon idea may come directly from a passage of Scripture, from a series of passages containing a basic unity or from a source located outside the confines of the Bible. If the sermonizer is directed to a passage of Scripture, then the study of its content and context should guide him to a subject which will be both the subject of the passage and the subject of his sermon. If the "sermon starter" came from a source outside the Bible, the sermonizer will then go to the Scriptures to determine the location and extent of coverage given to this idea within the context of Scripture. He must bear in mind the fact that his task is not to give good advice but rather as a preacher to present "good news."

Effective sermonizing demands that the preacher have a homiletical mind. Such a mind will make him aware of sermonic ideas as he reads and observes. It will also assist him in making all resources, general as well as specific, tributary to the work of sermonizing.

What constitutes a good preaching portion? It must be a passage which has logical unity. It must deal with one broad subject area. The requirement of logical unity will mean that the preaching portion will consist of one or more complete paragraphs since a good paragraph has one main idea. When one paragraph is used as the sermon base, the preaching points will often be obtained by the process of deduction. The general truth of the paragraph is established and then the sermonizer will move to the particulars within the paragraph. If a series of paragraphs are used as the base, the process of induction may be employed. Each paragraph will contribute its own idea. The sermonizer will then seek to determine the covering idea which unifies the paragraphs.

The boundaries of a preaching portion can often be determined by noting sudden shifts of style, tone, and content. References to new places and new persons will often give a clue to a thought transition.

Some passages of Scripture seem to have more homiletical possibilities than others. If a passage contains one or more of the following items, it may prove to be homiletically profitable. The following list is suggestive and not exhaustive.

1. A direct or indirect reference to a personal, community, or national *problem* needing solution.
2. A spiritual or social *practice* which should be encouraged or discouraged.
3. An *analogy* which when expanded will throw light upon some element of spiritual truth.
4. A spiritually *significant word* which, when clarified as to meaning, will provide help for the listener.
5. A *principle* or *precept* which needs amplification, illustration, or application.
6. An *evaluation of an item.*

It is wise for the preacher to bear in mind the fact that truth content is not in itself indicative of profitable preaching possibilities. It must be truth which has some practical meaning to the preacher and application for the anticipated listener. A sermon involves exposition plus application.

C. Studying a Preaching Portion

1. *Survey the Context of the Preaching Portion.*
   There are three steps involved in the process of surveying the context of the passage of Scripture which the sermonizer is using as a foundation for a sermon.
   a) *Survey the group of Bible books* in which your particular book is located. For example, if you were preaching on a passage in the Book of Ephesians, you would want to get a general grasp of the dates, emphases, and features of the four Prison Epistles of which Ephesians is one. A good Bible introduction text will provide helpful information at this point.
   b) *Survey the particular Bible book* in which your preaching portion is located.
      1) Discover the main theme of the Bible book. Read and reread it until the main teaching can be crystalized in your thinking.
      2) Learn what you can about the writer of the book. Some of this information may be discovered within the book itself but sometimes extra-Biblical sources will have to be consulted.
      3) Where was the book written?
      4) When was the book written?
      5) To whom was the book written?
      6) What prompted the original writing of the book?
      7) List any peculiar or important repeated terms.
      8) What does this book teach about God?
      9) What is the general tone of the book? Is it argumentation, exhortation, or instruction?
      10) Are there evidences within the book of manners and customs of those to whom it was first written?
      11) Formulate a broad, general outline of the book. Give special attention to changes of subject matter, personages, and places. Key phrases may help in the determination of this outline. Outstanding affirmations and reference to personal, church, or community problems may provide outline indicators.
      12) Compare several outlines which others have formulated to discover similarities in outline division.
   c) *Survey the immediate context* of the preaching portion. Dr. Charles Koller in his book, *Expository Preaching Without Notes*, has listed seven items which he terms factual data:
      1) Determine the *speaker* or *writer*. The type of person may give a valuable clue to the major thrust of the passage and its possible application.

2) Determine the *addressee*. The type of person or group who first received the message may be discovered in the congregation to which the preacher is scheduled to present his sermon.
3) Establish *an approximate* time for the incident or for the presentation of the original message. The homiletician will want to list other significant Biblical and extra-Biblical events which took place just before and just after.
4) Locate the *place* where the incident took place or where the passage was presented. It would be helpful to list other significant facts which took place at the same or nearby locations.
5) Clarify the *occasion* which prompted the contents of the Biblical passage. Similar conditions may exist in connection with the ones to receive the sermon based upon the passage.
6) Determine the *aim* or *purpose* behind the passage. Was this accomplished? Is that same aim or purpose relevant to the lives of the listeners today?
7) Formulate the *main theme* of the passage. This will be a phrase which summarizes its content.

Dr. Whitesell and Dr. Perry in their homiletical work, *Variety in Your Preaching*, have suggested two additional items.

8) Discover any recent *archaeological findings* which might have bearing upon the interpretation of this passage.
9) Note any *distinctive doctrines, ideas,* and *stylistic traits* of the Biblical writer which may provide helpful hints for the interpretation of the passage.

2. *Analyze the Content of the Preaching Portion*
   a) Read the passage in several translations. Each of the five following purposes may be pursued as the sermonizer reads the different versions. The unique findings from these readings should be recorded for possible inclusion within the sermon.
      1) To determine the *dominant impression* from the passage
      2) To discover the *major and minor personages* and that which is said about them
      3) To note significant *repeated words and phrases*
      4) To determine a *distinctive name or title* which might be given to the passage as a means of identification
      5) To prepare for the *public reading* of the passage from the pulpit.
   b) Formulate an *analytical outline* of the passage. The paragraph divisions will indicate possible breaking points for the outline.

No attempt should be made to rearrange the order of contents of the passage.
  c) Make a comparative study of *parallel passages*. Note any significant additions or deletions. This type of study will be especially relevant when preaching on the Gospels.
  d) Produce a *grammatical survey* of the preaching portion.
      1) The *diagramming of ideas* after the manner used in diagramming sentences in school English courses will help to clarify the logical relationships between ideas. This process is called thematic diagramming.
      2) Special attention should be given to the *punctuation marks*. A series of declarations, exclamations, or questions might provide preaching points.
      3) A study of the *etymology of words* will provide sermonic illustrative material. The meaning given in the dictionary can be made more relevant by checking the connotation of the word. The context often colors the meaning of the word.
      4) *Verb tenses* have greater significance in the Greek of the New Testament and the Hebrew of the Old Testament than in the English translations. Such translations as those by Montgomery and Williams will help the student who is handicapped at this point by not knowing the Greek language.
      5) A checking of the *word order* in the original language will clarify the emphasis within the sentence. In the Greek the emphatic words come first in the sentence.
      6) The Bible has an abundance of *figures of speech*. These figures should be identified and clarified as to their meaning and implications.
      7) *Repeated, peculiar, or distinctive terms* will not only provide sermonic illustrative material but may also provide bases for sermon points.

3. *Search the Content of the Preaching Portion for Sermon Ideas*
  a) Is the subject of the passage modified by one or more of the following interrogative adverbs: Why, how, when, or where? If such is the case, it may indicate that you should consider the modification sermonic process. (See pages 27-42.)
  b) Is the subject of the passage discussed from the standpoint of its nature? If such is the case, it may indicate that you should consider the clarification sermonic process. (See pages 42-51.)
  c) Is there a personal, community, or national problem cited directly or indirectly? If an answer, solution, or cure for the

problem is included, then you should consider the investigation sermonic process. (See pages 51–55.)

d) Are there key words or key word indicators within the passage? A key word is a plural noun which characterizes the main points of a message. A key word such as "reasons" may appear in the passage or a clause worded "because . . ." may indicate the key word "reasons." (See pages 27–29.)

e) Discover the one main idea of each paragraph. This may provide the substance of a main point of the message. The main idea of a paragraph may also give a hint as to the content of the sermon conclusion.

f) If your passage deals with an incident, discover the steps involved in the unfolding of it.

g) Familiar verses within the passage may provide sermonic ideas.

h) Is there a figure of speech within the passage? Be sure that you have a clear explanation of the meaning of the figure of speech before preparing your sermon.

i) Are there cause and effect relationships within the passage?

j) Is there a doctrinal emphasis within the passages?

k) Is there an activity emphasized which we should perform or avoid?

l) Is there an emphasis upon a chronological or geographical order?

m) What did this passage convey to the readers of past days?

n) As you have studied the passage, what practical advice have you gleaned for daily living?

The chart on page 23 shows the correlation of methodology between this book and that of an earlier work. The sermonizer should read and follow the methodology set forth in the *Biblical Sermon Guide* and read the indicated pages in *A Manual for Biblical Preaching* for additional guidance.

BIBLICAL SERMON GUIDE (1970)	A MANUAL FOR BIBLICAL PREACHING (1965)
The Modification Process Pages 27–42	The Foundational Pattern Pages 65-82
The Clarification Process Pages 42–60	
Sermon Type 1 Pages 43–44	The Analogical Pattern Pages 83-86
Sermon Type 2 Pages 44–45	The Etymological Pattern Pages 87-89
Sermon Type 3 Pages 45–46	
Sermon Type 4 Pages 46–48	The Illustrational Pattern Pages 99-101
Sermon Type 5 Pages 48–49	The Implicational Pattern Pages 101-105
Sermon Type 6 Pages 49–50	The Analytical Pattern Pages 90-95
Sermon Type 7 Pages 50–51	
The Investigation Process Pages 51–55	The Problematical Pattern Pages 95-98

II

ORGANIZATION OF THE OUTLINE FOR THE BIBLICAL SERMON

II. ORGANIZATION OF THE OUTLINE FOR THE BIBLICAL SERMON

A. The Sermonic Process of Modification

There are three basic sermonic processes which may be used in the construction of a sermon. These three are the process of *modification,* the process of *clarification,* and the process of *investigation.* The sermonizer has the task of selecting from these three the one which conveys the main thrust of the Bible passage on which he is speaking.

The sermonic process of modification involves qualifying, restricting, or limiting a subject in terms of one of *four interrogative adverbs.* These four interrogative adverbs are *"why," "how," "when,"* and *"where."* The interrogative "why" will provide the listener with a series of causes, purposes, reasons, and similar items. The interrogative "how" will provide the listener with a series of ways, means, methods, etc. The interrogative adverb "when" will indicate a series of times and the interrogative adverb "where" will indicate a series of places.

That which the sermon is to convey to the listener must be evident within the passage which forms the basis for the message. In fact, the preaching portion may provide material relating to more than one of the interrogative adverbs. In such a case, the sermonizer will select the one for his sermon which summarizes the most prominent thrust of the passage. He may at a later date preach a second sermon on the passage and use the material pertaining to a second interrogative which also had prominence in the passage.

The sermonizer must test the contents of the preaching portion to discover which interrogative is most prominent. This involves discovering whether or not certain key phrases summarize the support of the subject of the passage by its content. The following lists may serve as guides but are not exhaustive.

1. If the passage calls for support or acceptance of its subject because of one of the following *key phrases,* then the sermon will have the interrogative adverb "why" as its center. Each key phrase includes a key word (a noun in the plural which will characterize the main points of the sermon).

Because of:
Arguments set forth
Benefits to be derived
Bequests promised
Blessings to be received
Commands given
Dangers thereby avoided
Effects produced
Gains to be received
Guarantees provided
Honors to be bestowed
Imperatives given
Improvements to be wrought
Incentives offered
Injunctions set forth
Invitations extended
Issues at stake
Joys to be realized
Judgments to be rendered
Lessons which can be learned
Losses sustained
Needs manifested
Obligations placed upon us
Orders given
Penalties inflicted
Predictions made
Privileges offered
Profits to be gained
Reasons set forth
Results to be obtained
Rewards promised
Satisfactions to be gained
Values to be realized

2. If the passage provides support of its subject as indicated by one of the following *key phrases,* then the sermon will have the interrogative adverb "how" as its center.

By:
Avoiding blunders
Avoiding dangers
Avoiding excesses
Avoiding extremes
Avoiding the mistakes
Following instructions
Following the guides
Following the methods
Following the patterns
Following the plans
Following the practices
Following the prescriptions
Following the rules
Following the steps
Following the stipulations
Heeding admonitions
Heeding commands
Heeding the laws of —
Heeding the precautions
Heeding the sayings
Making adequate preparations
Making use of the provisions
Mastering details
Not giving way to one's fears
Obeying directives
Obeying injunctions
Obeying the teachings
Observing principles
Overcoming barriers
Practicing the fundamentals
Practicing the lessons
Surmounting obstacles
Taking advantage of the means provided
Taking advantage of the powers
Taking the better alternatives
Working within the systems

3. If the passage provides support of its subject by providing a *series of times,* then the sermon will have the interrogative "when" as its center. These may be seasons of the year, times of the day, months of the year, or periods in life.

4. If the passage provides support of its subject by providing a *series of area indications,* then the sermon will have the interrogative "where" as its center. These may be areas, groups, places, locations, positions, meetings, or regions.

NOTE: If one of these four tests does not indicate the major emphasis of the passage, then the process of modification should not be used.

The Eight Steps of the Modification Process

1. *Determine the subject*

The subject is the starting idea of the sermon. It should be the summarizing core of the preaching portion. The main thrust of the preaching portion must cover the major part of the passage. This will normally be discovered through induction. This general truth thus discovered will be the one from which one moves to particulars in the sermon development. The sermonizer should be able to prove that the subject which he determines for the passage is the one which is actually the one for that particular portion. This may sometimes be seen in the repetition of a core word.

When the preaching portion consists of one paragraph, the sermonizer should beware of selecting a subject which has been mentioned in only one or two verses as being the subject for the entire paragraph. The subject must cover the passage like a tent. If two or more paragraphs comprise the preaching portion, he must beware lest the subject of just one paragraph is selected as the major one for the several paragraphs.

One of the best ways to determine the subject is to read the portion which is to serve as the basis for the sermon and then to ask, "What is the main center of attention for this whole passage?" Such a center of attention may be a *doctrine* to study; a *duty* to perform; a *precept* or *maxim* to explore; a *problem* to solve; or an *occupation, profession,* or *calling* to pursue.

The subject of the preaching portion will become the subject for the sermon. It is general and broad in scope. There is the danger, however, of having it so broad that it misses the specific emphasis of the passage. "Prayer," for instance, is a worthy subject for a sermon, but if the passage deals basicly with a special type of prayer such as intercessory prayer, then this should be the subject. The sermonizer should watch for qualifying adjectives or nouns which tend to classify the subject. This same principle could be illustrated by the broad subject of tithing which might be classified or qualified by the word "storehouse," thus making the subject "storehouse tithing."

Subjects for sermons are normally one word or a short phrase. One exception to this occurs when there is a precept or maxim taken directly from Scripture or one formulated to convey truth which is in accord with Scripture. This precept or maxim will be in the form of a sentence.

The Bible is the best source for sermon subjects. There are occasions, however, when subjects will come from extra-Biblical sources. When the starting idea does come from one of these sources, the sermonizer should then turn to the Bible and locate the teaching within a Scriptural portion. This portion will consist of one or more paragraphs which treat the same subject as the one located in the extra-Biblical source.

There are passages of Scripture which may be more profitably taught in a Bible class than preached from a pulpit. A passage for preaching should have as its subject a matter of concern and importance which has relevance to the preaching purpose. It should capture the concern of the preacher in such a way that he feels that his listeners have a need for the subject. One of the tests of a sermon is that which happens to the man in the pew.

The following examples of sermon subjects will prove helpful when using the basic modification sermonic process:

1. Prayer
2. Intercessory prayer
3. God's work
4. Praying
5. Tithing
6. Soul winner
7. Discouragement

When the preacher has determined the subject of his preaching portion which in turn is to be the subject of his sermon, he will be wise at that point to gather information related to the subject. This process involves *surveying the subject*. The following ten questions will guide the sermonizer to material.

1. What have I read on the subject?
2. What have I observed which might throw light upon the subject?
3. What have I gleaned from the experience of the past on the subject?
4. What is the actual meaning of the subject?
5. What does the Scripture have to say on the subject?
6. What is my personal attitude or bias toward the subject?
7. What is the attitude or bias of my congregation toward the subject?
8. What famous quotations can I remember or locate pertaining to the subject?
9. What poetry can I recall which is related to the subject?
10. What is the real importance of the subject at this particular time?

2. *Formulate the Theme*

The preaching portion not only has a subject but also a theme.

Organization of the Outline

The theme is the specific aspect of the subject being dealt with in that passage. It will circumscribe the subject by pointing out the boundaries of its discussion.

The theme of the preaching portion will become the theme of the sermon. It will indicate by its wording the sermonic purpose. This could be referred to as the direction of the sermon. This direction may be *why, how, when,* or *where* as related to the subject. The sermon direction indicated at this point will establish the sermon interrogative.

Subject	Theme	Sermon Direction and Interrogative
1. Prayer	The profit of prayer	Why
2. Intercessory prayer	The necessity for intercessory prayer	Why
3. God's work	Supporting God's work	Why or How
4. Praying	Effective praying	How
5. Tithing	The ability to tithe	How
6. Soul winner	How to become a soul winner	How
7. Discouragement	Overcoming discouragement	How

The theme may be formed by adding a *modifier* to the subject: (Effective Praying). It may be formed by adding a *possessive* to the subject: (The Profit of Prayer, the Necessity of Intercessory Prayer, or the Qualifications of a Soul Winner). By adding a *verb of action* to the subject, one may form the theme: (Supporting God's Work or Overcoming Discouragement). The theme may be *indicative of a state of being:* (The Ability to Tithe).

When the theme has been determined, the sermonizer should *probe the theme* in order to clarify its meaning and to collect information concerning it. The following ten questions will aid in this analyzation process.

1. What was there in the preaching portion which led you to select this particular theme?
2. Are there terms in the theme which should be defined? This may be a necessary step both for the preacher and for the anticipated listeners.
3. Are there similes and metaphors which would throw light upon the theme?
4. What is your personal relationship to this theme?
5. What relationship would your anticipated audience have to this theme?
6. What statements of Scripture prove or strengthen this theme?
7. What relationship exists between each segment within the preaching portion and the theme?

8. Is this theme suitable for the time, place, and occasion?
9. Are there technical terms in the theme? If so, they should be explained and put into nontechnical forms.
10. Are there words in the theme which are employed in an unusual way?

3. *Construct a Proposition* (See page 90.)

The proposition occupies the focal point in the sermon outline. This part of the sermon has been referred to by different writers as the central idea, the controlling assertion, the statement, the big truth, the subject sentence, and the thesis. It is this sentence which is the integrating center of the sermon. It promotes stability of structure, unity of thought, and forcefulness of impact.

The proposition announces the theme in sentence form. It proclaims the truth which the sermonizer desires to establish and apply. The good proposition is one which embodies the principle or most striking truth of the Scriptural portion on which the man is preaching. Great preaching is always in the present tense. It must speak to the concerns of the day in the thought forms and language of the day. It is important, therefore, that this sentence be true to the impact of Scripture and also that it be relevant to human experience. The proposition must be stated in the form of a *timeless truth* which was valid for Bible times and is still valid for the day in which it is being preached. Since it is a timeless truth, no proper names other than that of deity will be included within it.

There are *three types of propositions:*
1. A statement of *evaluation* or *judgment*
   Example: Praying is profitable.
2. A statement of *obligation* or *duty*
   Example: It is necessary for Christians to engage in intercessory prayer.
   Christians should support God's work.
3. A statement of *activity without stated obligation*
   (The emphasis is upon ability.)
   Example: We can become more effective in praying.
   Every Christian can tithe.
   A Christian can overcome discouragement.

4. *Establish a Transitional Sentence*

We are now ready to construct a *rhetorical bridge* between the core of the sermon (the proposition) and the development of the sermon (the body). This rhetorical bridge is a transitional sentence which gathers that which has preceded it in the sermon and makes the logical transition to that which is to follow.

The sermonizer looks at the proposition (the theme in sentence form) which he has just established and determines which of the following six questions this sermon should answer for the listener.

1. How can I...
2. Why should I...
3. When should I...
4. Where should I...
5. Where can I...
6. Why is it...

The *interrogative adverb* from the preceding questions is now taken as the sermonic interrogative. This sermonic interrogative or its substitute will be used in the transitional sentence.

Interrogative
a. How
b. Why
c. When or Where

Interrogative Substitute
by (plus a verbal)
because of
in which or at which

The interrogative or interrogative substitute is followed in the transitional sentence by a key word. This key word is always a plural noun which will characterize the main points of the message. The type of key word to be used is determined by placing the sermonic interrogative in front of the proposition and thus forming a question. The sermonizer then selects a plural noun which will provide a logical answer to the question which he has just formed. (See example below.)

The sermonizer is now ready to put the three parts of the transitional sentence together. These *three parts* consist of the *proposition* (as much of it as possible), the *interrogative* (or interrogative substitute) and the *key word*. This transitional sentence contains the three items which tie the parts of the sermon together logically. It will be referred to a number of times in the delivery of the sermon and should be constructed with care. It should be worded so that the preacher will feel at ease as he gives it to his congregation. It is for this reason that he may want to use an interrogative substitute in place of the simple interrogative. He may also find it advantageous to put the key word into a phrase. (See page 27.) It should be noted that the key word or key phrase will always follow the interrogative or interrogative substitute.

If the sermon is being constructed on one specific passage of Scripture, this reference should be noted in the transitional sentence.

Example:

Proposition: A nation can become prosperous.

[The two following items (the formulated question and answer) are sermonic construction steps. They do not appear on the finished outline.]

(How can a nation become prosperous?)
(By obeying *commands*)

Transitional Sentence: A nation can become prosperous

by obeying the commands of God as set forth in Deuteronomy 6:1-25.

Note: "By obeying" is the interrogative substitute for the interrogative "how."

"The commands of God" is the key phrase.

"Deuteronomy 6:1-25" is the preaching portion upon which the sermon is based.

5. *Develop Main Divisions* (See page 91.)

The main points of a sermon serve to amplify, explain, or prove the proposition. There will normally not be more than five and never less than two. The sermonizer will seek to make the points clear and concise in construction as well as in presentation. They must be noted, pondered, and remembered by the listener.

The form and content of the points will be controlled by the key word. All of the main points in a message are characterized by a noun in the plural appearing in the transitional sentence as the key word. Each point should contain a single idea. These ideas should be drawn from the preaching portion. If the sermon is using a starting idea from an extra-Biblical source, then each main point will be derived from the extra-Biblical sermon base but be undergirded as well from Scripture. This Scriptural undergirding is important. (See Chapter III D.)

There are certain rules of grammar and structure which should be observed since they enhance the quality of style and aid the memory of both the preacher and listener. The points should be *parallel in grammatical form* when possible. The visual memory of the preacher will be aided when he *underlines the points.* Figurative language should be *avoided* since it does not prosper understanding. The points should be arranged with the people to whom they are presented in mind. The purpose behind the presentation will also have an influence upon their order.

A Scriptural undergirding should be placed at the end of each main point. This will consist of the Bible book, chapter, and verse reference which substantiate the main point. That part of the verse should be written after the reference which says Biblically that which the main point includes.

Example:

    I. *Remember God.* Deut. 6:12: "Then beware lest thou forget the Lord...."

   II. *Love God.* Deut. 6:5: "And thou shalt love the Lord thy God...."

  III. *Declare God.* Deut. 6:6-7a: "And these words which I command thee this day shall be in thine heart: and thou shalt teach them diligently..."

IV. *Serve God.* Deut. 6:13: "And thou shalt fear the Lord thy God and serve Him...."

6. *Amplify the Main Divisions into Subdivisions*

Amplification is the process of using subdivisions which will amplify and explain the main points of the message. There will be at least two and normally not more than five of these under each main point. The first one in the series may well serve the purpose of clarifying the meaning of any term in the main division which needs clarification. The last one in the series will always be one of application to the immediate congregation. Since it is desired that these subdivisions be remembered by the listener, it is important that they be short in form, few in number, and similar in form. As many of the subdivisions as possible should be drawn from the passage upon which the sermonizer is basing his message.

The simplest method of obtaining subdivisions is to take one of the six interrogative words (how, why, when, where, who, or what) and apply this word to the main point. A question will thus result which the subdivision should answer. More than one subdivision can be gleaned by applying a single interrogative.

Subdivisions may be obtained by making an exposition of the main point. This may take the form of exposition by definition. There may be definition by the giving of synonyms, by putting the item in its correct classification, by giving the etymology of a word, or by telling what the main point is not.

The main point can be amplified by narration. This is the process of presenting a series of events in story form. These may be illustrations of the main division. It will involve putting into word picture form persons and objects, thus telling how persons or things look, feel, or act. If the main division is an incident, it may be unfolded by following these four steps:
1. Establish the setting and get the action started.
2. Develop the main body of the incident.
3. Bring the incident to its logical climax.
4. Draw the conclusion which may well be a logical application for the listener.

A main point can sometimes be developed by using the process of thought categorization. These are certain patterns of thinking which, when recognized and followed, will aid in establishing a logical unfolding of an idea. Among the general categories that may be applied as guides in the homiletical development of an idea are the following:
1. If the main point involves a *person,* this person may be sketched as to heredity, environment, development, capacity, character, career, achievement, and reputation.
2. If the main point is an *event,* this may be examined with re-

gard to time, place, antecedents, consequences, human participation, and evidences of divine providence.
3. If the main point involves *relationships,* these relationships may be itemized as being in relation to self, neighbor, and God.
4. The *time order* may be applied to the main point showing its relation to the past, present, and future.
5. The category of *source, nature,* and *effect* may be used.
6. If one is considering a Biblical *miracle of healing,* he may survey the case, cause, cure, and consequence.
7. The category of *size* or *dimension* involves breadth, length depth, and height.
8. The category of *social relationships* involves husbands and wives, children and parents, servants and masters.
9. The category of *spiritual status* includes saints and sinners, preconversion and postconversion.
10. The *spiritual development* category might include the call, commission, conduct, and compensation.

Each of the main divisions should have a Bible book, chapter, and verse designation after it which we have termed the Scriptural undergirding. This Scriptural undergirding should say in Biblical wording that which is stated as the main division in the phraseology of the sermonizer. Words and phrases within this Scriptural undergirding may warrant exposition. Each of these may form the basis for a subpoint. As this exposition is developed, the meaning of the main division will thereby be clarified.

Beyond these methods of interrogation, definition, narration, thought categorization, and exposition of the Scriptural undergirding there are some additional helps listed under the sermon types involving clarification as listed on pages 42 to 51 of this guide.

7. *Formulate an Introduction* (See pp. 91–92.)

The introduction is that part of the sermon which clarifies the reason for this audience to listen to this preacher discuss this subject on this occasion. It is composed of an introductory approach sentence followed by an outlined section, and finally by a sermonic explanation.

In formulating the *approach sentence,* the sermonizer should select a word or idea within the proposition which needs definition, clarification, or amplification. This word or idea will become the core of the entire introduction. This core thought of the introduction should be developed in terms of the daily living of the listeners. It should, therefore, meet the people where they are living. The sermon will later lead them to the cross for salvation, sanctification, or service. The sermon thus begins with a secular discussion of the word or phrase selected from the proposition.

The *outlined section* of the introduction will consist of a development of the approach sentence. It should be kept in mind that the introduction is designed to point the listeners to the truth to be developed within the body of the sermon. The sermonizer should avoid the insertion of material within the introduction which might tend to divert the listener's attention from the main message of the sermon. The time used by the introduction should occupy no more than fifteen percent of the speaking time for the entire message.

The *sermonic explanation* is inserted within the sermon outline as the final segment of the introduction. It is the sermonic bridge between the secular segments of the introduction and the body of the sermon which is to follow. This explanation will put the sermon into its Biblical context. It will involve drawing certain material from the Bible study itself which will be helpful to the listener as he listens to the message. Only that material should be included, however, which is relevant to the unfolding of the message. The explanation will also include any unique features of the type of sermon being presented. This will help to prepare the listener to follow its development.

The following positive characteristics should mark the introduction. It should be brief, clear, appropriate, unified, purposeful, varied, and audience-centered. It should be presented in a friendly, tactful, and direct manner in order to stimulate the interest of the listeners.

Such items as flattery, apologies, and items of complexity should be avoided. Technical language within the introduction will tend to short-circuit the listening of the audience. It is not wise to reveal the main points of the sermon within the first part of the message. The exception to the rule would occur when the material to be discussed in the message is of a complex nature or when the audience is by nature and circumstance not alert to follow the step-by-step development of the message. Material, whether humorous or serious, which is not relevant to the sermon at hand should be avoided. The introduction is not an end in itself but points to that which is to come.

Example:

Introduction: Prosperity has its price. (Approach sentence)

(Outlined section)
1. Prosperity: "A thriving condition, good fortune, success."
2. "Watch lest prosperity destroy generosity." H. W. Beecher

Explanation: 1. (Show that the subject and theme of the sermon are inherent within the preaching portion.)

2. (Point out features of the content and context of the preaching portion which may have interest value as far as the theme is concerned.)
3. (Show the significance of the type of sermon as related to Scripture, the occasion, and the congregation.)

8. *Determine the Conclusion* (See pp. 92–93.)

The conclusion is the summarization of the sermon showing its relevance to the daily living of the listeners. It will challenge the listeners to make some decision regarding the content of the message.

There are two parts to a conclusion. The first of these is the *objective sentence* which is the first sentence of the conclusion. It is formulated by beginning with "Therefore, we [the ones to whom the message is addressed] should. . . ." This introduction to the sentence will be followed by the response anticipated or desired by the speaker. This response will consist of a combination of the proposition of the sermon and the purpose behind the presentation of the message.

The objective sentence is then followed by the second part of the conclusion consisting of an *outlined section*. This outlined section may consist of a recapitulation of the main points or of the applications made throughout the sermon. These may be paraphrased or put into epigrammatic form. The sermonizer may choose to list a series of specific ways in which the suggested applications made within the sermon can be specifically applied to the lives of the listeners. He may want to challenge the hearers to accept the points made in the message through appealing to altruism, aspiration, curiosity, duty, fear, love, or reason. (See *Expository Preaching Without Notes* by Dr. Charles Koller, Baker Book House, p. 132). If the main points of the message have been stated as negatives, the preacher should then employ a positive conclusion. The message should be ended on a positive note. If the preacher is aware of the fact that several may be erecting within their minds certain objections to giving a favorable response to his message, he may want to list those anticipated objections and provide a positive answer for each rather than letting the listener establish these as unanswered mental objections.

The conclusion must be concise. If it is too long, interest will tend to lag. No material should be inserted in the conclusion which is not relevant to the thrust of the message. The conclusion is not the place for an apology, joke, or humorous remark. Do not give the congregation the impression that you are about to conclude your message when such is not the case. It is not necessary nor is it wise to give a formal statement to the listener that the conclusion is now approaching. Prepare the conclusion with care and make certain that it is a

Organization of the Outline

conclusion for that specific message rather than one of broad generalities.

THE LOGICAL RELATIONSHIP OF THE PARTS OF A SERMON OUTLINE

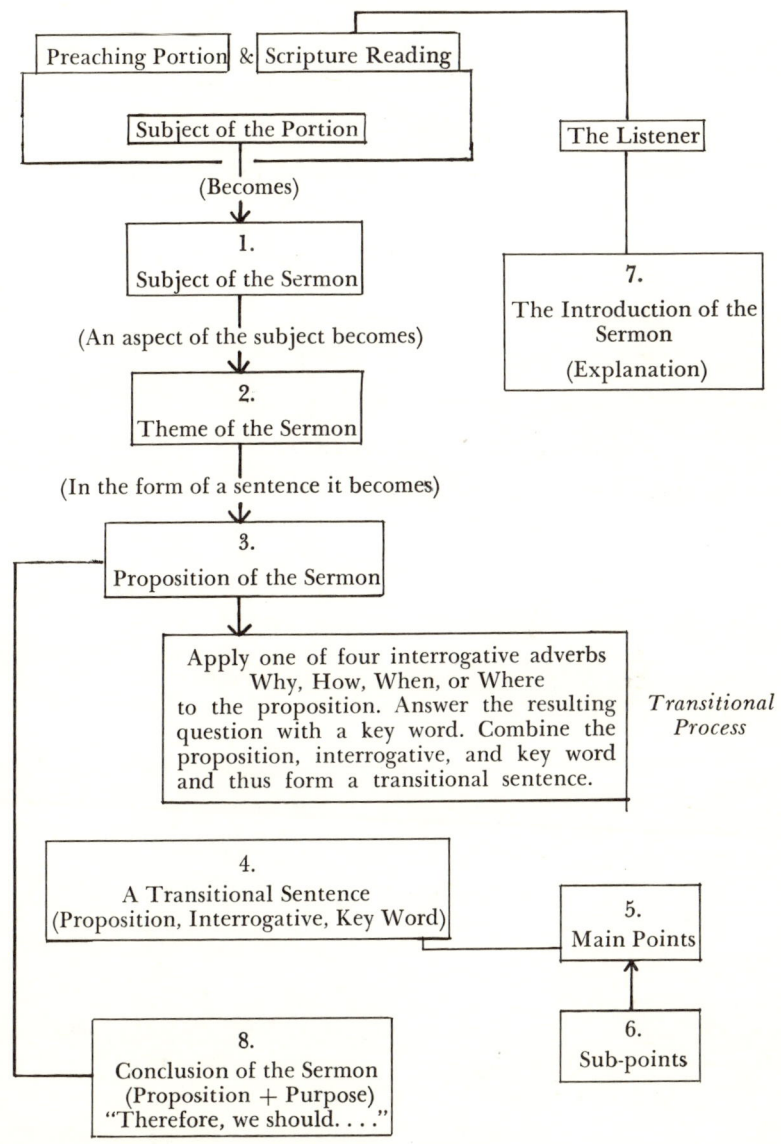

THE SCRIPTURAL FOUNDATION OF THE PARTS OF A SERMON

Sermon Title: *Obedience Brings Prosperity*
Sermon Subject: *Prosperity*
Sermon Theme: *How to become prosperous*

Preaching Portion	Main Points / Subpoints		
Deut. 6:1-25	Key word: *Commandments* ....Vs. 1		
Vs. 1. _____			
Vs. 2. _____		Vs. 2	Vs. 2
Vs. 3. _____	Main Points	Subpoints	Vs. 3
Vs. 4. _____			
Vs. 5. (1) (2) (3)	II. Love God	1.	
Vs. 6. _____		2.	
Vs. 7. (1) (2) (3)	III. Declare God	3.	Vs. 6
(4) (5)		4.	
Vs. 8. (6) (7)		1. 5.	
Vs. 9. _____		2.	
Vs. 10. _____		3.	
		4.	
Vs. 11. _____		5.	Vs. 10
Vs. 12. (1)	I. Remember God	6.	
Vs. 13. (1) (2)	IV. Serve God	7.	
Vs. 14. (4)		1.	
Vs. 15. (5)		1.	
Vs. 16. _____		2.	
Vs. 17. (3)		3.	Vs. 17
Vs. 18. _____			Vs. 18
Vs. 19. _____			
Vs. 20. _____			Vs. 20
Vs. 21. _____			
Vs. 22. _____			
Vs. 23. _____			
Vs. 24. _____		Vs. 24	Vs. 24
Vs. 25. _____	*Conclusion*	Vs. 25	Vs. 25

Subject: Prosperity *Preaching Portion:* Deut. 6:1-25
Theme: How to Become Prosperous *Sermonic Process:* Modification

OBEDIENCE BRINGS PROSPERITY

Intro.: Prosperity has its price.
    1. Prosperity: "A thriving condition, good fortune, success."
    2. "Watch lest prosperity destroy generosity" H. W. Beecher.
Explanation:
    1. (Show that the subject and theme of the sermon are inherent within the preaching portion.)
    2. (Point out features of the content and context of the preaching portion which may have interest value as far as the theme is concerned.)
    3. (Show the significance of the type of sermon as related to Scripture, the occasion, and the congregation.)
Prop.: A nation can become prosperous.
T.S.: A nation can become prosperous by obeying the commands of God as set forth in Deut. 6:1-25.

  I. *Remember God.* Deut. 6:12: "Then beware lest thou forget the Lord. . . ."
     1. (Each subpoint is related to the main point under which it is listed. It does *not* refer to the preceding subpoint.)
     2.
     3.
     4. (Subpoint of application)
    (Ill.) Danger of prosperity

 II. *Love God.* Deut. 6:5: "And thou shalt love the Lord thy God...."
     1. (As far as possible, undergird each subpoint with Scripture.)
     2.
     3. (Subpoint of application)
    (Ill.) Song: Love of God

III. *Declare God.* Deut. 6:6-7a: "And these words which I command thee this day shall be in thine heart: and thou shalt teach them diligently. . . ."
     1.
    (Ill.) Tephilim
     2.
     3.
     4.

5. (Subpoint of application)
IV. *Serve God.* Deut. 6:13: "And thou shalt fear the Lord thy God and serve Him. . . ."
    1.
    2.
    (Ill.) Exod. 17:1-7
    3. (Subpoint of application)

Concl.: Therefore, we as a nation should seek to become prosperous. Deut. 6:25 "And it shall be our righteousness, if we observe to do all these commandments before the 'Lord our God, as He hath commanded us."
    1. Rememer God
    2. Love God
    3. Declare God
    4. Serve God

' B. The Sermonic Process of Clarification

The second of the three sermonic processes is that of clarification. This process is used when the sermonizer desires to make his subject more clear and understandable. He wants to help his listeners see the nature, meaning, or identity of the subject. In the first process interrogative adverbs provided the key to the process; but in this process of clarification, one of two interrogative pronouns is emphasized. These two are "what" and "who."

How can a sermonizer know that a passage of Scripture will provide material for a sermon developed by the process of clarification? There are several indicators which may provide help at this point.

1. Is there an *analogy* within the passage which could be used to clarify the meaning of a spiritual concept?
2. Is there an *English Bible word* within this and several other passages of Scripture which could be clarified in meaning by checking the Greek and/or Hebrew words of which it is a translation?
3. Is there reference in the passage to *a doctrine,* the meaning of which could be clarified by showing evidences of its application to daily life?
4. Is there a *statement of principle,* the meaning of which could be amplified and clarified by giving illustrations of its truth?
5. Is there a *verse of Scripture* where implications and inferences based upon its words and phrases will amplify its meaning?
6. Is there an *experience* or *process* which can be clarified by citing the parts or steps involved in it?

7. Does the passage make reference to a *group of individuals* whose personal identification should be clarified to make the passage more meaningful as a sermonic foundation?

One of the following key words or a synonym will characterize the main points of the message:
1. For an analogy use *comparisons* or *similarities*.
2. For a word study use *definitions*.
3. For a doctrinal declaration use *evidences* or *applications* (suppositions, hypothesis, statements, or observations).
4. For a statement of principle use *illustrations*.
5. For a verse of Scripture use *implications* or *inferences*.
6. For an incident or process use *parts* or *steps*.
7. For the identification of persons use *individuals* or *groups*.

The development of a sermon by this process will often take the sermonizer beyond the confines of a single portion of Scripture.

Sermon Type 1: By Developing an Analogy or Comparison

Aim: To clarify the meaning of a spiritual concept
Procedure: By developing an analogy or comparison
Type of Sermon: This might be called an analogical (See *Manual for Biblical Preaching**, pp. 83-86) or pictorial sermon (See p. 65).
Key words: *Comparisons* or *similarities*
Sermon Items:
1. The *subject is the spiritual concept.*
2. The *theme* consists of the key word (comparisons) followed by the spiritual concept and finally the physical part of the analogy.
3. The *proposition* is the statement of the analogy or comparison.
4. The *transitional sentence* will include the key word (comparisons) followed by the theme and the purpose for clarifying the analogy.
5. The *main points* will be statements of comparison between the physical and spiritual portions of the analogy.
6. The *subpoints* may be formulated by having the *first* one develop the physical portion of the main point, the *second* one develop the spiritual aspect of the main point, and the *third* one emphasize the practical application of the main point.
7. The *conclusion* may summarize the applications which have been made throughout the sermon.
8. The *introduction* should stress the significance of the physical part of the analogy in the life of the past and the present. The explanation will emphasize the nature of an analogy and

---
* Hereafter referred to as *Manual*

the place and prominence of this one within the context of Scripture.

Examples:
Heb. 12:1-17
Subject: Living the Christian life
Theme: Comparisons between living the Christian life and running a race
Proposition: Living the Christian life is like running a race.
Transitional Sentence: The following comparisons between living the Christian life and running a race will help to clarify how we ought to live.
Sample Main Point: Just as it is wise to avoid hindrances when one is running a race, so it is wise to avoid hindrances when one is living a Christian life. Hebrews 12:1b, "Let us also lay aside every weight and sin which clings so closely. . . ."

Matt. 5:13
Subject: The nature of the Christian life
Theme: Comparisons between the nature of the Christian life and the nature of salt.
Proposition: The nature of the Christian life is like the nature of salt.
Transitional Sentence: The following comparisons between the nature of the Christian life and the nature of salt will help clarify what our Christian life should be like.
Sample Main Point: As salt acts to stop the spread of physical decay so the Christian should be a force to stop the spread of spiritual decay.

Sermon Type 2: By Providing Definitions for a Significant English Bible Word

Aim: To clarify the meaning of a significant English Bible word
Procedure: By providing definitions of that word
Type of Sermon: This might be called an etymological (see *Manual,* pp. 87-89) or word study sermon.
Key Word: *Definitions*
Sermon Items:
1. The *subject* is the English Bible word. This word must be the English Bible translation of two or more Greek and/or Hebrew words. It is important that these words be enough different in meaning from one another that they can form the basis for mutually exclusive main points.
2. The *theme* consists of the key word (definitions) followed by the subject.

ORGANIZATION OF THE OUTLINE 45

3. The *proposition* puts the subject into a doctrinal or ethical declaration. This should be worded so that a definition of the subject could be inserted within the proposition.
4. The *transitional sentence* includes the key word (definitions) followed by the subject, and the purpose for clarifying the meaning of the English Bible word.
5. The *main points* will be definitions of the English Bible word which have been derived from studying the Greek and/or Hebrew words of which it is a translation.
6. The *subpoints* may include a discussion of the word picture behind the Greek or Hebrew word, references to the occurrence and significance of the word and the application of the particular definition of the word to the daily life of the listener.
7. The *conclusion* may summarize the definitions and their applications.
8. The *introduction* may emphasize the occurrence and significance of the English Bible word in daily life and Scripture. The explanation will emphasize the practicality of studying words.

Example:
  Subject: Forgiveness
  Theme: Definitions of forgiveness
  Proposition: God forgives sin
  Transitional Sentence: A study of the definitions of the English Bible word "forgive" will help to clarify what is involved in God's forgiving sin.
  Sample Main Point: The English Bible word "forgive" in Ps. 78:38 is the word "Kophar" meaning "to cover." "But He, being full of compassion forgave their sin."
  (Note: There are other methods of defining than by the use of the Greek and Hebrew equivalents. This particular method is developed here due to its emphasis upon Bible content. With slight variations, this method may include other forms of definition.)

Sermon Type 3: By Giving Applications of a Doctrinal Truth

Aim: To clarify the meaning and significance of a doctrinal declaration

Procedure: By giving evidences of the application of this doctrinal truth to the daily life of the listener

Type of Sermon: This might be called a suppositional (see p. 66) or roman candle sermon (see p. 66).

Key Words: *Evidences* or *Applications*

Sermon Items:

1. The *subject* is the doctrinal word or phrase.
2. The *theme* consists of the key word (evidences or applications) followed by the doctrinal word or phrase.
3. The *proposition* puts the doctrinal word or phrase into the form of a doctrinal declaration.
4. The *transitional sentence* includes the key word (evidences or applications) followed by the subject and the purpose for clarifying the meaning and significance of the doctrine.
5. The *main points* will include the doctrinal declaration and an evidence or application of its truth to daily living.
6. The *subpoints* will include a development of the main point together with a pointed application of that main point to daily life.
7. The *conclusion* has no unique features.
8. The *introduction* may define the doctrine in practical everyday terms. The explanation will clarify the place of this particular doctrine within the total doctrinal framework. It will also clarify the prominence of this doctrine within the confines of Scripture.

Example: Jonah 1
Subject: The sovereignty of God
Theme: Evidences of the sovereignty of God
Proposition: God is sovereign
Transitional Sentence: A study of the evidences of God's sovereignty will help to clarify the practical value of the doctrinal truth.
Sample Main Point: The doctrinal teaching that God is sovereign is evidenced in His designation of His workers. Jonah 1:1, "Now the word of the Lord came unto Jonah. . . ."
(Note: There may be instances where the key words "suppositions," "hypotheses," "statements," or "observations" may be used to clarify the meaning of a doctrinal truth.)

Sermon Type 4: By Giving Illustrations of a Principle

Aim: To clarify the meaning and practicality of a statement of principle
Procedure: By giving illustrations which visualize and apply its truth
Type of Sermon: This might be called an illustrational (see *Manual*, pp. 98-101) or practical sermon (see p. 65).
Key Word: *Illustrations*
Sermon Items:
1. The *subject* is the statement of principle. This statement may

be a direct statement of Scripture, based upon a verse of Scripture or in accord with the import of the teaching of Scripture.
2. The *theme* consists of the key word (illustrations) followed by the statement of principle (subject) and the verse of Scripture upon which it is based.
3. The *proposition* is the statement of principle.
4. The *transitional sentence* will include the key word (illustrations) followed by the purpose for illustrating this particular statement of principle.
5. The *main points* will include the statement of principle with the verse of Scripture upon which it is based followed by the identification of the particular illustration which forms the basis for this point. The illustration will be identified as to content and verse location.
6. The *subpoints* may be arranged after the pattern of the steps used in telling a story since each point directs the attention to a narrative incident. The final subpoint in the series should apply the truth of the statement of principle to the particular area of life indicated by the illustration which forms the core of the main point.
7. The *conclusion* has no unique features.
8. The *introduction* should center its attention upon the discussion of one of the thought-carrying words in the proposition. This discussion should center in the daily life of the listeners. The explanation will discuss the context of the Scripture text.

Examples:

Subject: You can be certain that sin will be discovered.
Theme: Illustrations of the principle that you can be certain that sin will be discovered as set forth in the verse, "Be sure your sin will find you out" (Num. 32:23).
Proposition: You can be certain that sin will be discovered.
Transitional Sentence: By studying the illustrations of this principle, we will be more convinced of its scope of truth.
Sample Main Point: The principle that you can be certain that sin will be discovered as set forth in Num. 32:23; "Be sure your sins will find you out," is illustrated in the experience of David and his sin against Bathsheba in II Sam. 11.

Subject: It is tragic to avoid responsibility.
Theme: Illustrations of the principle that it is tragic to avoid responsibility as seen in the life of Saul who "hid himself among the stuff" (I Sam. 10:22).
Proposition: It is tragic to avoid responsibility.
Transitional Sentence: By seeing illustrations of this principle, we will be encouraged to accept all valid responsibility.

Sample Main Point: The principle that it is tragic to avoid responsibility as set forth in the life of Saul and the verse, "Behold he hath hid himself among the stuff," is illustrated as one like Saul avoids his responsibility to his nation (I Sam. 10:22b).

(Note: It is possible to develop this method by induction rather than deduction. In such a case, the sermonizer takes the outstanding incidents within the life of an individual and then seeks to discover a principle of life which would give sermonic unity to the incidents.)

Subject: It is wise to be true to your trust.
Theme: Illustrations of the principle that it is wise to be true to your trust
Proposition: It is wise to be true to your trust.
Transitional Sentence: By surveying illustrations of this principle in the life of Joseph, we will see more clearly the wisdom of adopting this as our principle of life.
Sample Main Point: The principle that it is wise to be true to your trust is illustrated in the life of Joseph in his dealings with his parents (Gen. 37:1-36).

Sermon Type 5: By Drawing Inferences from Words and Phrases

Aim: To clarify and amplify the meaning of a verse of Scripture
Procedure: By drawing implications or inferences from words or phrases within the verse
Type of Sermon: This might be called a jewel (see p. 64), facet (see page 64) or inferential sermon (see pp. 64–65).
Key Words: *Implications* or *Inferences*
Sermon Items:
1. The *subject* is the verse of Scripture. This verse should be one which is loaded with meaning.
2. The *theme* consists of the key word (inferences or implications) followed by the verse of Scripture.
3. The *proposition* is the verse of Scripture.
4. The *transitional sentence* will include the theme followed by the purpose for expanding the meaning of the verse. This purpose will include a rephrased summary of the major emphasis of the verse.
5. The *main points* will include the verse of Scripture followed by the key word (inferences or implications) and the wording of that which the key word represents. The final item in the main point is the word or phrase from the verse which gives the Scriptural basis for the point.

Organization of the Outline

6. The *subpoints* will include a development of the main point and a practical application of its truth to daily living.
7. The *conclusion* has no unique features.
8. The *introduction* should present to the listeners the need for considering the truth included within this verse of Scripture. The explanation will show the relationship of this verse to its context.

Example:
  Subject: "God is our refuge and strength, a very present help in trouble."
  Theme: Implications of the verse, "God is our refuge and strength, a very present help in trouble."
  Proposition: "God is our refuge and strength, a very present help in trouble."
  Transitional Sentence: The implications drawn from the words in this verse of Scripture will help us understand some of the greatness of God's provision for us.
  Sample Main Point: "*God is our refuge and strength, a very present help in trouble,*" contains the implication that this truth is centered in a person, "God."

Sermon Type 6: By Showing the Development of a Spiritual Truth

Aim: To clarify the relationship between the parts of an experience or steps of a process and the spiritual theme which the incident or process was meant to convey

Procedure: By using parts of an experience or steps in a process to show the development and comprehensiveness of a spiritual truth

Type of Sermon: This might be called an analytical (see p. 63 and *Manual,* pp. 90-95) or a pictorial sermon (see p. 65).

Key Words: *Parts* or *Steps*

Sermon Items:
1. The *subject* is the identification of the incident or process by name and Scriptural location.
2. The *theme* indicates that the sermonizer is going to analyze the subject.
3. The *proposition* includes the theme followed by the purpose behind the analysis.
4. The *transitional sentence* includes the theme followed by the key word (parts or steps) and the purpose behind the analysis.
5. The *main points* include an identified part of the incident or step in the process and the aspect of the purpose behind the analysis which it clarifies.

6. The *subpoints* will include a development of the main point and a practical application of its truth to the daily experience of the listener.
7. The *conclusion* has no unique features.
8. The *introduction* relates the purpose behind the analysis to the daily life of the listener. The explanation throws light upon the context of the incident or process.

Example:
Subject: The incident of the healing of the man born blind as recorded in John 9:1-41
Theme: The analysis of the incident of the healing of the man born blind as recorded in John 9:1-41
Proposition: An analysis of the incident of the healing of the man born blind as recorded in John 9:1-41 will provide us with information as to how God works.
Transitional Sentence: An analysis of the incident of the healing of the man born blind as recorded in John 9:1-41 into its component parts will provide us with information as to how God works.
Sample Main Point: The description of the individual healed of his blindness as given in John 9:1-6 shows us that Christ works by grace.

Sermon Type 7: By Identifying Individuals or Groups

Aim: To clarify the identity of the individuals or groups included within a plural or collective personal noun or pronoun
Procedure: By giving specific identification of the individuals or groups represented by a plural or collective personal noun or pronoun
Type of Sermon: This might be called an analytical sermon. (See p. 63.) (See *Manual,* pp. 90-95.)
Key Words: *Individual* or *Groups*
Sermon Items:
1. The *subject* may be a duty, doctrine, precept, problem, occupation, profession, or calling.
2. The *theme* unites the plural or collective personal noun or pronoun with the subject.
3. The *proposition* puts the theme into the form of a declaration of purpose.
4. The *transitional sentence* includes the key word followed by the proposition.
5. The *main points* will stress one of the individuals or groups included in the proposition.
6. The *subpoints* have no distinctive features.

7. The *conclusion* should stress motivation.
8. The *introduction* should clarify the subject.

Example:
Subject: Tithing
  Theme: Church members and tithing
  Proposition: Church members should practice tithing.
  Transitional Sentence: The following individuals within the church membership should practice tithing.
  Sample Main Point: The pastor should practice tithing.

C. The Sermonic Process of Investigation

1. *The Discussion of a Problem*

The sermonic process of investigation involves the examination of a problem in detail in order to discover a possible solution, cure, or answer. This type of sermon has been referred to by some as a question sermon (see p. 66) and others have referred to it as a chase technique sermon (see p. 63). This type of sermon originates in the experience of the people to whom it is preached. This type of preaching has an initial advantage in that it presents something for which a need is felt.

This whole approach to preaching has a close kinship to the pedagogy advanced by John Dewey. In the Dewey methodology there are five steps, namely: (1) a felt difficulty, (2) location and definition of the difficulty, (3) suggestion of possible solutions, (4) development by reasoning of the suggested solutions, and (5) further observations and exploration leading to acceptance or rejection of the solution.

Several designations have been given to this challenge of preaching on problems. The following list of designations, writers, and homiletics books will provide sources in which the interested sermonizer may find additional help.

Designation	*Author*	*Book*
Life Situation Preaching	Luccock	*In the Ministers Workshop*
	Blackwood	*Preparation of Sermons*
	Jordan	*You Can Preach*
	Caldwell	*Preaching Angles*
	Kemp	*Life Situation Preaching*
Problem Solving Preaching	Caldwell	*Preaching Angles*
Bifocal Preaching	Cleland	*Preaching to Be Understood*
Personal Problem Preaching	Gibson	*Planned Preaching*
Pastoral Preaching	MacLennan	*Pastoral Preaching*
	Coffin	*What to Preach*

Designation	Author	Book
Counseling Preaching	Linn	*Preaching as Counseling*
Therapeutic Preaching	Oates	*The Christian Pastor*
Preventive Preaching	Jefferson	*The Minister as Prophet*
	Jefferson	*The Minister as Shepherd*
Ethical Preaching	Hoppin	*Office and Work of the Christian Ministry*
	Brastow	*Work of the Preacher*
Social Preaching	McCracken	*The Making of the Sermon*

The book entitled *Discussion in Human Affairs* written by James McBurney and Kenneth Hance provides a process used when discussing a problem. This discussion process is related to John Dewey's reflective thinking concept and is also basic to this sermonic process of investigation. There are three basic types of problems which one may discuss. The first is that of a problem of fact, such as: What is Christianity. The second type is that of a problem of value, such as: Is honesty the best policy? The third type of problem is one of policy and can be illustrated by the question: What can be done to promote missions in the local church? This whole process involves diagnosis, description, and prescription.

2. *The Development of the Sermonic Process*

Biblical preaching has some unique purposes which distinguish it from the general secular discussion of a problem. The discussion process has, therefore, been adjusted to meet the needs of the Biblical sermon. The outstanding feature is the special emphasis placed upon the Biblical solution to the problem. It is actually a miniature sermon in itself. (Compare pages 54ff. and 58ff.) About one-third of the entire preaching time should normally be occupied with the presentation of this Biblical solution which is located in the fourth main point of the message.

The sermonizer should develop his sermon outline by formulating the following eight items in sequence.

1. The *subject* is the problem which he is investigating.
2. The *theme* includes the purpose of investigation and the subject.
3. The *proposition* is the statement of the need to find a solution, cure, or answer for the problem.
4. The *transitional sentence* involves the statement of the procedure to be followed and the purpose of investigation. There is no need for using a key word in this sermonic process because the nature of the main points is specified in accordance with the investigative process.
5. The *main points* are four in number and are formulated as questions. These are the questions which need to be answered

Organization of the Outline

if one is to investigate a problem and find a solution, cure, or answer.
1) *What is the problem?*
2) *How prevalent is the problem?*
3) *What have been some of the proposed solutions to the problem?*
4) *What passage of Scripture makes constructive contributions toward a solution, cure, or answer for the problem?*

6. The *subpoints* provide answers to the questions which comprise the main points.
7. The *introduction* should establish the need for finding a solution, cure, or answer for the problem. There will be a strong emphasis upon the presence of the problem in the daily experience of the listeners.
8. The *conclusion* will summarize the development of the fourth main point in the body of the message. It will reiterate the main emphases in the Biblical solution, cure, or answer to the problem.

Example:

Subject: The problem of discouragement

Theme: An investigation of the problem of discouragement

Proposition: There is a need for finding a solution to the problem of discouragement.

Transitional Sentence: A discussion of the problem of discouragement in terms of daily experience and Scriptural guidance will help us in our search for a possible solution.

Main Points:

I. *What is the problem?*
   This can be developed by defining, limiting, and diagnosing the problem. The definition may be by negation, classification, etymology, context, illustration, or by giving synonyms. The limitation of the problem may come because of the character of the audience, the occasion, and the possible area of its application. The problem may be diagnosed by giving symptoms, causes, and effects.

II. *How prevalent is the problem?*
    The development of this point will note the prevalence of the problem in the reading, listening, and working experience of the preacher and his people. It will show the occurrence of the problem in Scripture as a whole and in specific sections of Scripture. The listener should realize after hearing the development of this section of the sermon that since it is so prominent he should be concerned about it.

III. *What have been some of the proposed solutions to the problem?*
The development of this point will be comprised of a series of solutions which extra-Biblical writers have advanced. The nature, source, and sponsor of each proposal will be noted. This will enable the listener to check for himself at a later date if he so desires. It will also show the listener that the preacher has done some research on the problem before preaching upon it. A fair evaluation of each proposal should be given to the listener.

IV. *What passage of Scripture makes constructive contributions toward a solution, cure, or answer for the problem?*
The development at this point in the sermon could comprise a sermon in itself. No less than two or more than five suggestions will be made for solving the problem. It is preferable to have these suggestions drawn from one segment of Scripture. Each suggestion will be documented by chapter and verse. It is important to make certain that the sermonic solution to the problem is related to the same problem within the Scriptural context.

A caution should be given at this point pertaining to the use of the sermons written according to the sermonic process of investigation. The preacher must make certain that adequate emphasis is placed upon the Scriptural contributions. Some congregations will appreciate that as much as three-fourths of the sermon preaching is given to the fourth point and its development.

Subject: The problem of discouragement
Theme: An investigation of the problem of discouragement
Preaching Portion: I Kings 19:1-21
Sermonic Process: Investigation

A CURE FOR DISCOURAGEMENT

Intro.: Discouragement seems to vary in direct proportion to the frequency with which we follow local and world news.
  1.
  2.
Prop.: There is a need for finding a cure for the problem of discouragement.
T.S.: A discussion of the problem of discouragement in terms of daily experience and Scriptural guidance will help us in our search for a possible cure.

  I. *What is the problem?*

ORGANIZATION OF THE OUTLINE 55

      1. How would you define it? "Discouragement is the state of being depressed, dejected, and hopeless" (American College Dictionary).
      2. What are its limits, effects, and possible causes?

II. *How prevalent is the problem?*
      1. In Scripture
      2. In present day living

III. *What have been some of the proposed cures for the problem?*
(Each subpoint will be a proposed solution.)
Where did you read or hear about the solution?
Who advocates it?
What do you think of its merits or weaknesses?

IV. *What passage of Scripture makes constructive contributions toward a cure for the problem?*
Explanation: Show the relationship between the problem and the passage which in this case is I Kings 19:1-18.
      1. *Make certain that you are prepared physically.* I Kings 19:4-8. Vs. 8, "And he arose, and did eat and drink and went in the strength of that meat forty days and forty nights. . . ."
(Insert subpoints)
      2. *Make certain that you are prepared spiritually.* I Kings 19:9-14. Vs. 12b, ". . . and after the fire a still small voice"; Vs. 13b, ". . . what doest thou here, Elijah?"
(Insert subpoints)
      3. *Make certain that you are involved in service.* I Kings 19:15-18. Vs. 15, "And the Lord said unto him, Go, return on thy way to the wilderness of Damascus. . . ."
(Insert subpoints)
      4. *Make certain that you are ready to work with others.* I Kings 19:19-21. Vs. 19, "So he departed thence, and found Elisha . . . and cast his mantle upon him.
(Insert subpoints)

Concl.: Therefore, we as Christians should take these steps as outlined in I Kings 19 in order that we might overcome discouragement.
      1. Get ready physically   3. Get involved in service
      2. Get ready spiritually   4. Be ready to work with others

D. The General Process of Sermon Outlne Organization

1. *Style, Illustrations, and Title*

1) *Arrange the sermonic items* formulated in the sermonic process of modification, clarification, or investigation according to the sermon pattern for that particular process. (See pp. 41–42, 54–55 and 58–60.)
2) *Check the sermonic items for style.*
   a. Four items within the outline must be complete sentences.
      1 The *approach* sentence which is the first sentence in the introduction.
      2 The *proposition* which is the sermon in a sentence.
      3 The *transitional* sentence which is the sermonic bridge between the proposition and the points.
      4 The *objective* sentence which is the first sentence of the the conclusion.
   b. The introduction including the explanation and the conclusion should be in outline form.
   c. Make certain that the main points of the message agree in content and form with the key word.
   d. Ascertain whether or not it is possible to have the main points of the message parallel in form. Such an arrangement will aid the speaker in delivery and aid the listener in hearing and remembering the message.
   e. Be sure that under each of the main points of the message there is at least one subpoint of application. This will often be the final one in the series.
   f. The main points of the message should be underlined.
   g. Follow the sermonic pattern for indentation of sermon items thus leaving as much white space on the outline as possible.
   h. The entire outline should be on one side of one sheet of paper.
3) *Add illustrative material* where it is needed for "throwing light upon" the content of the message. (See pp. 93–94.)
   a. Only one illustration should be used for a single idea.
   b. The illustrations should be relevant, plausible, and in good taste.
   c. Different types of illustrations should be used.
   d. Select the illustrations from a variety of sources.
4) *Formulate a title.* This should be selected in keeping with the mood of the sermon, the nature of the audience, and the content of the message. It should not contain more than four thought-carrying words. The title should provide bulletin-board appeal and a means for filing the message after it has been presented.

2. *Questions for Checking the Sermon Outline*

Organization of the Outline

1) *Title:*
    Is it indicative of the content of the sermon?
    Is it in accord with the preaching task?
    Is it interesting?
2) *Introduction:*
    Does it meet the listeners where they live?
    Is there a word or phrase in the approach sentence which is also in the proposition?
    Is it in outline form?
    Explanation:
        Does it give evidence of careful research?
        Does it include specifics rather than generalities?
        Have you shown that the subject of the sermon is also the subject of the preaching portion?
        Have you pointed out the unique features of this particular type of sermon?
        Have you shown the relevancy of each item to the main thrust of the sermon?
3) *Proposition:*
    Is it a complete sentence?
    Is it a timeless truth? (It should not contain a name other than that of deity.)
    Have you avoided the use of figurative language?
    Have you avoided including a plural noun which might be mistaken by the listener to be a key word?
4) *Transitional Sentence:*
    Are you sure that it consists of three parts?
        As much of the proposition as possible?
        A key word (noun in the plural)?
        An interrogative or an interrogative substitute?
    Have you checked the meaning of the key word in the dictionary?
    Does this key word actually characterize the main points in form and in content?
5) *Main Points:* (Minimum of two and maximum of five)
    Are you certain that all of the words are needed?
    Did they all come from the preaching portion?
    Are they all either positive or negative?
    Does each one have adequate Scriptural undergirding?
        (Books, chapter, verse, and portion of the verse)
    Are they mutually exclusive?
    Does each contain only one idea?
    Have you avoided figurative language?

Does the Scriptural undergirding give substantiation for the point?
6) *Subpoints:* (Minimum of two and a maximum of five)
    Does each one have a logical relationship to the main point under which it is listed?
    Does each one add to the progression of thought?
    Have you obtained as many of them as possible from the preaching portion?
    Is there at least one subpoint of application under each main point?
    Have you included Scriptural undergirding for as many as possible?
    Have you worded each in the best way to be remembered?
7) *Conclusion:*
    Is it in outline form?
    Have you included any material which is not relevant to the rest of the sermon?
    Is it evident that you have given careful consideration to the preparation of the conclusion?
    Have you given clear indication of the action which you desire the listeners to take as a result of hearing this message?
8) *General Items:*
    Are you certain that your preaching portion consists of one or more complete paragraphs?
    Do you have a minimum of four complete sentences in the outline?
        The approach sentence (first sentence of introduction)
        The proposition
        The transitional sentence
        The objective sentence (first sentence of conclusion)
    Have you used only numbers (not letters) to designate your main points and subpoints?
    Are you sure that you have only one illustration for an idea?
    Are there any words in the outline which could be omitted without sacrificing clarity?
    Have you used several different types of illustrations? (See *Manual*, p. 81.)

A Cure for Discouragement

Subject: Discouragement
Theme: Overcoming Discouragement
Preaching Portion: I Kings 19:1-21
Sermonic Process: Modification

Intro.: "All discouragement is from the devil" (Quote from Catherine Marshall)
    1. Discouragement and our daily living
    2.
    3.
   Explanation:
    1. (Show relationship between I Kings and discouragement)
    2. (Show the prevalence of discouragement within the Scripture)

Prop.: A Christian can overcome discouragement.
T.S.: A Christian can overcome discouragement by following the steps outlined in 1 Kings 19:1-18.

  I. *Make certain that you are prepared physically.* I Kings 19:4-8
    Vs. 8 "And he arose, and did eat and drink and went in the strength of that meat forty days and forty nights . . ."
    1.
    (Ill.)
    2.
    3.
    4. (Show how the truth of the main point may be applied to the immediate congregation.)

 II. *Make certain that you are prepared spiritually.* I Kings 19:9-14
    Vs. 12b ". . . and after the fire a still small voice"
    Vs. 13b ". . . What doest thou here, Elijah?"
    1.
    2.
    (Ill.)
    3.
    4. (Show how the truth of the main point may be applied to the immediate congregation.)

III. *Make certain that you are involved in service.* I Kings 19:15-18
    Vs. 15 "And the Lord said unto him, Go, return on thy way to the wilderness of Damascus . . ."
    1.
    2.
    3.
    (Ill.)
    4. (Show how the truth of the main point may be applied to the immediate congregation.)

IV. *Make certain that you are ready to work with others.* I Kings 19:19-21 Vs. 19 "So he departed thence, and found Elisha . . . and cast his mantle upon him."
    (Ill.)

　　　　1.
　　　　2.
　　　　3.
　　　　4. (Show how the truth of the main point may be applied to the immediate congregation.)
Concl.: Therefore, we as Christians should take the necessary steps to overcome discouragement.
　　　　1. Get ready physically　3. Get involved in service
　　　　2. Get ready spiritually　4. Be ready to work with others

III

VARIATION OF THE OUTLINE FOR THE BIBLICAL SERMON

III. VARIATION OF THE OUTLINE FOR THE BIBLICAL SERMON

A. By Using a Different Sermon Structure

1. *Adverbial Sermon* or *Interrogative Sermon*
   This sermon structure involves the division of the subject or text by the application of several interrogative words. Such words as who, what, why, where, and how are often used.
   Blackwood, *The Preparation of Sermons*, p. 149.
   Mark, *Patterns for Preaching*, pp. 82-96.
   (Main Points)
   I. *What* is prayer?
   II. *Who* should pray?
   III. *Why* should we pray?

2. *Analytical Sermon* (See, p. 49.)
   This sermon structure uses as its main divisions the various parts of the text or preaching portion. The sermon outline follows the pattern of the analysis of the passage.
   Mark, *Patterns for Preaching*, pp 67-71.
   (Main Points)
   I. The case of the blind man   John 9:1-6
   II. The cure of the blind man   John 9:7-15
   III. The consequences   John 9:16-41

3. *Chase Technique Sermon* or *Guessing Game Sermon* (See, p. 51.)
   This sermon explores a problem in pursuit of a solution. The sermon structure consists of a series of questions and answers related to the problem.
   Jones, *Principles and Practice of Preaching*, pp. 106, 107.
   Luccock, *In the Minister's Workshop*, pp. 143-145.

4. *Couplet Sermon*
   This sermon structure is composed of two related parts. The first consists of the exhortation and the second is the promise or practice. The two main divisions of the sermon come from the two parts of the text. It is a textual sermon. (See, p. 67.)
   Mark, *Patterns for Preaching*, pp. 98-102.

5. *Devotional Sermon*
   This is a meditation on a Bible passage. There is no real outline. There is also very little exegesis represented within it. The sermon actually consists of running comments.
   Littorin, *How to Preach the Word with Variety*, pp. 68-70.

6. *Dramatic Continuity Sermon* (Similar to a play)
   This sermon structure is composed of three parts which, as steps, provide a dramatic action. The first step is exposition, the second is complication, and the third is resolution.
   Caldwell, *Preaching Angles*, pp. 78-80.
   Davis, *Design for Preaching*, pp. 182-184.
   Jordan, *You Can Preach*, pp. 231-133.
   Stidger, *Preaching Out of the Overflow*, pp. 107-110, 114, 115.
   (Main Points)
   I. Exposition
   II. Complication
   III. Resolution or Solution

7. *Facet Sermon* or *Jewel Sermon* (See p. 48.)
   This sermon takes one idea and then shows by relationships and applications the relevance of this idea to experience. The faceting process may involve emphases of origin, consequences, implications, or concrete instances.
   Luccock, *In the Minister's Workshop*, p. 137.
   Sangster, *The Craft of the Sermon*, pp. 87-92.
   I. Origins ———————┐ An ┌——— III. Instances
   II. Implications ——————┤ Idea ├——— IV. Consequences

8. *Hegelian Sermon* or *Three Point Sermon*
   This sermon structure has three main divisions. The first states the thesis, the second states its opposite or the antithesis, and the third states the synthesis or truth which emerges from the conflict of points one and two.
   Blackwood, *The Preparation of Sermons*, pp. 148, 149.
   Jones, *Principles and Practice of Preaching*, p. 106.
   Jordan, *You Can Preach*, pp. 226-238.

9. *Inductive Sermon*
   This sermon builds from particulars. It begins with experience and then gradually builds toward and finally arrives at the Biblical conclusion.
   Blackwood, *The Preparation of Sermons*, pp. 143-145.
   Sangster, *The Craft of the Sermon*, pp. 84-87.
   (Main Points)
   I. Experience A   The spiritual truth
   II. Experience B   which is the common
   III. Experience C   denominator

10. *Inferential Sermon* or *Deductive Sermon* or *Implicational Sermon* (See p. 48.)
    This sermon is one in which the text is the subject and the dis-

cussion is a series of inferences drawn directly from the text. It is the process of deducting certain truths from a text.
   Hogg, *A Handbook of Homiletics and Pastoral Theology*, pp. 57-59.
   Marks, *Patterns for Preaching*, pp. 87-89.
   Pattison, *The Making of the Sermon*, pp. 72-75.
   Phelps, *Theory of Preaching*, p. 31.

11. *Ladder Sermon* or *Telescopic Sermon* or *Oratorical Sermon* or *Pyramid Sermon*
    This sermon structure is one in which each main division grows out of or builds upon the previous point. Each point carries the subject out a little farther like the unfolding of a telescope or the climbing of a ladder. A form of the sermon can be used when seeking to give a panoramic view of Scripture pertaining to one great truth. As an oratorical sermon, it is planned toward a climax.
      Jones, *Principles and Practice of Preaching*, pp. 104, 105.
      Littorin, *How to Preach the Word with Variety*, pp. 71-75.
      Luccock, *In the Minister's Workshop*, pp. 134-137.
      Mark, *Patterns for Preaching*, pp. 129-131, 145-148.
         (Main Points)
         I. Point I
         II. Point I plus an addition
         III. Point II plus an addition

12. *Objections Answered Sermon*
    This sermon seeks to answer the objections which the listener may have in mind as he hears the message. These are the objections which might keep him from accepting the truth of the sermon or performing the activity advocated.
    Each main point is a possible objection which the listener may advocate in opposition to the thrust of the message. The sub-points answer the anticipated objections.
      Mark, *Patterns for Preaching*, pp. 48-54.

13. *Pictorial Sermon* (See pp. 43, 49, and 84-85.)
    The divisions of this sermon structure are based upon the parts of the picture being described.
      Mark, *Patterns for Preaching*, pp. 120-124.

14. *Practical Sermon* (See pp. 46-48.)
    This sermon is one in which each main point contains a separate and distinct application of the truth of the text.
      Mark, *Patterns for Preaching*, pp. 93-95.

15. *Propositional Sermon* or *Pilgrimage Sermon*

This sermon structure is one in which the proposition clearly states the subject and the task which the sermon proposes to accomplish. This proposition is a statement made for consideration, proof, or acceptance. The pilgrimage sermon consists of a series of progressive related propositions.
Jordan, *You Can Preach*, pp. 229-230.
Mark, *Patterns for Preaching*, pp. 78-81.
Montgomery, *Preparing Preachers to Preach*, p. 136.
(This is the modification process of this *Biblical Sermon Guide* or the foundational pattern of the *Manual for Biblical Preaching*.)

16. *Question Sermon* (See p. 51.)
This is a sermon where each point is in the form of a question.
Jones, *Principles and Practice of Preaching*, pp. 103, 104.

17. *Roman Candle Sermon (Similar to a Facet Sermon — See p. 64.)* (See p. 45.)
This sermon structure consists of a series of statements or observations related to the truth under consideration. The number of points is not intended to exhaust the subject.
Jones, *Principles and Practice of Preaching*, pp. 105-106.
Luccock, *In the Minister's Workshop*, pp. 141, 142.

18. *Skyrocket Sermon*
This sermon begins at the ground level of life and then soars to spiritual truth which has meaning for a situation. At that point, separate observations or suggested actions are elucidated.
Luccock, *In the Minister's Workshop*, p. 14.

19. *Suppositional Sermon* (See p. 45.)
The divisions of this type of sermon structure are the various suppositions or hypotheses which are to be proved or disproved by the subdivisions.
Mark, *Patterns for Preaching*, pp. 57-60.

20. *Surprise Package Sermon*
This sermon is one which, when it gets started and gradually develops, seems to be heading in a certain direction. It then takes an unsuspected turn into another direction.
Luccock, *In the Minister's Workshop*, pp. 142, 143.

21. *Symphonic Sermon*
This sermon is built around a couplet which is repeated throughout the sermon until it is locked into the memories of the hearers.
Caldwell, *Preaching Angles*, pp. 43-48.
Jones, *Principles and Practice of Preaching*, pp. 113, 114.

Jordan, *You Can Preach*, pp. 228-229.
Stidger, *Preaching Out of the Overflow*, pp. 105-107.

22. *Synthetical Sermon*
    This type of sermon takes a group of ideas or texts and constructs them into a complete unity.
    Fry, *Elementary Homiletics*, p. 15.
    Mark, *Patterns for Preaching*, pp. 61-63.

23. *Textual Sermon, Microscopic Sermon, Natural Sermon or Comprehensive Sermon* (See pp. 48–49, Sermon Type 5.)
    This sermon is one in which the text is divided and the main divisions of the sermon are suggested by words and phrases of the text. The points or divisions are often on the surface of the text. The order of the points may or may not follow the order of the words within the text.
    Broadus, *On the Preparation and Delivery of Sermons*, pp. 293-298.
    Caldwell, *Preaching Angles*, pp. 28-48.
    Etter, *The Preacher and His Sermon*, pp. 201-203.
    Gibbs, *The Preacher and His Preaching*, pp. 237-243.
    Hogue, *A Handbook of Homiletics and Pastoral Theology*, pp. 43-45.
    Hoppin, *Homiletics*, pp. 465-468.
    Kidder, *A Treatise on Homiletics*, pp. 201-206.
    Littorin, *How to Preach the Word with Variety*, pp. 47-50.
    Mark, *Patterns for Preaching*, pp. 71-74, 95-98.
    Pattison, *The Making of the Sermon*, pp. 64-71.
    Riley, *Preacher and His Preaching*, pp. 74, 75.
    Ripley, *Sacred Rhetoric*, pp. 109-120.
    Sangster, *The Craft of the Sermon*, pp. 68, 69.
    Whitesell, *The Art of Biblical Preaching*, pp. 47-51.
    Whitesell & Perry, *Variety in Your Preaching*, pp. 36, 37, 43-45.

24. *Twin Point Sermon*
    This sermon has two divisions which set forth opposing or contrasting aspects of one truth or one word of Scripture.
    Luccock, *In the Minister's Workshop*, pp. 140, 141.

B. By Using Different Biblical Subject Matter

1. *Admonitions*
    Eph. 5:1-32 – Live According to Your Calling
    Heb. 10:32-39 – Keep Your Confidence

2. *Affirmations*

This type of sermon keeps reaffirming the doctrines in which we believe.
Jordan, *You Can Preach*, pp. 221-223.
Josh. 7:16-26 — A Great Confession
Matt. 6:33 — The Supreme Object of Human Endeavor
Luke 13:1-5 — Repent or Perish
I John 5:1-5 — Victorious Faith

3. *Analogies* (See pp. 43–44.)
This type of sermon develops a Biblical analogy.
Caldwell, *Preaching Angles*, pp. 103-105.
Luccock, *In the Minister's Workshop*, p. 142.
Mark, *Patterns for Preaching*, pp. 54-57, 120-124.
Stidger, *Preaching Out of the Overflow*, p. 207.
Isa. 64:6 — Fading as a Leaf
Matt. 5:13-16 — The Influence of a Good Man
II Cor. 5:1-21 — Ambassadors for Christ
Heb. 12:1-17 — The Race of Life
Rev. 22:16 — The Bright and Morning Star

4. *Antithetical Segments*
This sermon has been named a combinational sermon.
Mark, *Patterns for Preaching*, pp. 107-110, 124-129.
Prov. 10:1-22 — Sharp Contrasts
Heb. 10:11-15 — Once and Forever

5. *Apocalyptic Passages*
This type of sermon deals largely with eschatology. The predictions are usually couched in visions of images, living creatures, birds, cities, and battles which are employed as symbols of that which is being foretold.
Perry, *Manual for Biblical Preaching*, p. 136.
Rev. 1:8 — The Alpha and Omega
Rev. 17:14 — The Lamb

6. *Apostasies*
Exod.. 32:1-35 — Who Is on the Lord's Side?
Judg. 2:1-5 — The Place of Weeping
II Tim. 3:1-12 — Times of Stress
II Peter 2:1-21 — The Inroads of Error

7. *Battles*
Perry, *Manual for Biblical Preaching*, p. 117.
Josh. 7:1-26 — Defeated by One Man
II Sam. 5:17-25 — The Message of Marching Feet

8. *Beatitudes*
Perry, *Manual for Biblical Preaching*, p. 123.

VARIATION OF THE OUTLINE 69

    Ps. 32:1, 2 — Blessed Forgiveness
    Ps. 41:1-3 — The Blessedness of the Compassionate
    Isa. 32:20 — Blessed Are the Sowers
    John 20:29 — Blessed Are the Believers
    Graham, William, *The Secret of Happiness*. Garden City, New York: Doubleday and Co., Inc., 1955, p. 117.
    Dunbar, John W., *The Beatitudes of the Old Testament*. Cincinnati: Jennings and Graham, p. 235.

9. *Benedictions*
    Gen. 27:27-30 — A Family Benediction
    Ruth 2:4 — A Labor Day Benediction
    II Cor. 13:14 — A Trinitarian Benediction
    II Thess. 3:16 — The Benediction of Peace
    Jude 24, 25 — To God Be the Glory
    Rev. 22:21 — The Benediction of Grace

10. *Biographies*
A biographical sermon grows out of the facts concerning a Biblical character as these throw light upon the man in the pew.
Baxter, *Speaking for the Master*, pp. 42-43.
Blackwood, *Preaching From the Bible*, pp. 52, 93.
Burrell, *The Sermon: Its Construction and Delivery*, pp. 96-101.
Caemmerer, *Preaching for the Church*, pp. 171-173.
Caldwell, *Preaching Angles*, pp. 49-72.
Etter, *The Preacher and His Sermon*, pp. 219-221.
Gibbs, *The Preacher and His Preaching*, pp. 257-261.
Jones, *Principles and Practice of Preaching*, pp. 111, 112.
Littorin, *How to Preach the Word with Variety*, pp. 95-103.
Mark, *Patterns for Preaching*, pp. 26-30.
McComb, *Preaching in Theory and Practice*, pp. 83-87.
Montgomery, *Preparing Preachers to Preach*, p. 133.
Ray, *Expository Preaching*, pp. 65-68.
    Gen. 6:9-22 — Noah, A Builder According to God's Specifications
    Luke 23:26-49 — The Crowd at the Cross
    Rom. 16:1-27 — God's Gallery of Grace
    Col. 1, 4 — Epaphras, The Ideal Pastor
Fickett, Harold L., Jr., *Profiles in Clay*. Los Angeles, Calif.: Cowman Publishing Co., Inc., 1963, p. 147.
McPherson, Anna Talbott, *Forgotten Saints*. Grand Rapids, Michigan: Zondervan Publishing House, 1961, p. 113.
Sockman, Ralph W., *Men of the Mysteries*. New York: Abingdon Press, 1927, p. 197.

Stevenson, Herbert F., *A Galaxy of Saints*. Westwood, New Jersey: Fleming H. Revell Co., 1958, p. 158.

Whyte, Alexander, *Our Lord's Characters*. Bible Characters, Vol. VI. London: Oliphants Ltd., n.d.

11. *Births*
    Gen. 5:28-31 – Child of Grace
    I Sam. 1:1-28 – Asked of the Lord
    Matt. 1:18-25 – God With Us
    Luke 1:57-66 – What Then Will This Child Be?

12. *Character Sketches*
    This involves the presentation of the essential traits or qualities of the individual. It reflects the inner life which determines the outer life and events involving the individual.
    Davis, *Design for Preaching*, pp. 97-105.
    Mark, *Patterns for Preaching*, pp. 31-35.
    Perry; *Manual for Biblical Preaching*, p. 108.
    Matt. 3:1-17 – John the Baptist, a Voice in the Wilderness
    Acts 8:1-40 – Philip, a Dedicated Deacon
    Acts 16:11-18 – Lydia, a Godly Business Woman
    Acts 18:24-28 – Apollos, a Powerful Preacher

13. *Churches*
    Rev. 2:1-7 – Leaving the First Love
    Rev. 2:8-11 – The Poor Rich Church
    Rev. 2:12-17 – The Dangerous Minority
    Rev. 2:18-29 – Love Without Orthodoxy
    Rev. 3:1-6 – A Form or a Force?
    Rev. 3:7-13 – Vigilance, the Price of Victory or The Faithful Few
    Rev. 3:14-22 – Riches to Rags
    McDaniel, George, *The Churches of the New Testament*. George H. Doran Co., New York, 1921, 299 pages.
    Morgan, G. C., *Letters of Our Lord*. Pickering & Inglis, Ltd., London, 109 pages.

14. *Commandments*
    Exod. 20:1-17 – Lessons for Living
    John 13:21-35 – The Eleventh Commandment
    Chappell, Clovis G., *Ten Rules for Living*. New York: Fleming H. Revell Co., 1923, p. 159.
    Flowers, H. J., *The Permanent Value of the Ten Commandments*. London: George Allen and Unwin Ltd., Ruskin House, 1927, p. 283.
    Massee, J. C., *The Gospel in the Ten Commandments*. New

VARIATION OF THE OUTLINE 71

York: Fleming H. Revell Co., 1923, p. 159.
Morgan, G. Campbell, *The Ten Commandments*. New York: Fleming H. Revell Co., 1901, p. 126.
Pearson, Roy, *The Hard Commands of Jesus*. New York: Abingdon Press, 1957, p. 125.
Strauss, Lehman, *The Eleven Commandments*. New York: Loizeaux Brothers, 1955, p. 174.

15. *Comparisons*
    This is termed a comparative sermon and it involves a study of a comparison or contrast. The text is examined to discover a resemblance or unlikeness of persons, conditions, attitudes, or courses of action.
    Luke 10:38-42 — The Good Portion
    Luke 18:9-14 — Two Ways to Pray

16. *Contributions of Bible Characters*
    Perry, *Manual for Biblical Preaching*, p. 110.
    Exod., Num., and Deut. — Moses made contributions in the areas of law, literature, and religion.
    II Kings 22:1 — 23:30 — A Reign to Remember
    Acts — Paul made contributions in the areas of missions, literature, and church life.

17. *Conversations*
    Caldwell, *Preaching Angles*, pp. 105-108.
    Perry, *Manual for Biblical Preaching*, p. 121.
    Gen. 3:1-7 — A Beguiling Conversation
    Matt. 4:1-11 — A Tempting Conversation
    Luke 7:1-10 — The Discovery of a Great Faith
    Macartney, Clarence E., *Great Interviews of Jesus*. New York: Abingdon Press, 1944, p. 190.

18. *Conversions*
    Perry, *Manual for Biblical Preaching*, p. 129.
    Luke 19:1-10 — From Limb to Land
    John 4:1-42 — Drink and Never Thirst Again
    Acts 8:26-40 — Crossroads in the Desert
    Acts 9:1-31 — A New Life
    Acts 16:25-40 — A Song Before the Dawn

19. *Covenants*
    Gen. 12:1-3 — The Abrahamic Covenant
    Gen. 9 — The Rainbow for a Sign
    Gen. 15 — More than the Stars
    Gen. 26 — A Promise Not Forgotten
    Josh. 24:1-28 — A Tarnished Covenant

II Sam. 7:4-16 – Davidic Covenant

20. *Crises*
Isa. 6 – Indelible Impressions
Luke 19:41-44 – Tears in the Midst of Triumph
Lehman, Louis Paul, *Tears of the Bible*. Grand Rapids, Michigan: Zondervan Publishing House, 1958, p. 93.

21. *Doctrinal Material*
This sermon may deal with an entire doctrine as seen in Scripture or with one aspect of a doctrine as seen in the entire Bible or section of the Bible. Be sure to study the natural divisions of a doctrine before preaching on it.
Blackwood, *Doctrinal Preaching for Today*, p. 224.
Breed, *Preparing to Preach*, pp. 427-446.
Broadus, *On the Preparation and Delivery of Sermons*, pp. 59-66.
Mark, *Patterns for Preaching*, pp. 40-44.
McCracken, *The Making of the Sermon*, pp. 45-47.
Montgomery, *Preparing Preachers to Preach*, pp. 137-139.
Perry, *Manual for Biblical Preaching*, p. 125.
Wood, *The Preacher's Workshop*, pp. 50-53.
Isa. 7:1-16 – Fact not Fiction
Rom. 8:1-17 – Life in the Spirit
I Cor. 15:1-58 – Not in Vain
Heb. 7:1-26 – Our Great High Priest

22. *Dramatic Scenes*
This sermon is based upon a passage of Scripture which exhibits a picture of human life. The sermon is also referred to as pictorial. (See p. 65.)
Davis, *Using the Bible in Public Address*, pp. 84-96.
Mark, *Patterns for Preaching*, pp. 120-124.
Gen. 22:1-19 – The Blessing of Obedience
Exod. 3:1-6 – The Bush Is Burning Again
Exod. 12:1-36 – A Day to Remember
I Kings 18:17-40 – The Fire of the Lord Fell

23. *Epitaphs*
Exod. and Num. – Aaron, the Great Compromiser
II Chron. 29-32 – Hezekiah, the Purifier of Religion
Acts 15-18 – Silas, an Answer to Inadequacy
II Tim. 4:1-18 – Demas, the Deserter
Macartney, Clarence Edward, *Bible Epitaphs*. New York: Abingdon Press, 1936, p. 200.

24. *Family Life Experiences*

Perry, *Manual for Biblical Preaching*, p. 112.
   I Sam. 1:9-20 — Secrets of a Great Mother
   I Sam. 3:10-18 — A Father Who Failed
   Eph. 5:22-23 — Wives and Husbands
   Eph. 5:22 — 6:4 — Happy Homes
   Eph. 6:1-4 — Children and Their Parents
   Col. 3:1-4:1 — Home Harmony

25. *Figures of Speech* (See pp. 43-44.)
    Gen. 4:1-15 — The Voice of Blood
    I Cor. 3:10-15 — No Other Foundation
    I Cor. 3:16-23 — God's Temple
    I Cor. 12:1-31 — The Church: The Body of Christ
    Minear, Paul S., *Images of the Church in the New Testament*. Philadelphia, The Westminister Press, 1960, p. 294.

26. *Fires*
    Gen. 19:24-29 — Consuming Fire
    Gen. 22:1-14 — Behold, the Fire and the Wood
    Lev. 10:1-7 — Offering Strange Fire
    Dan. 3:1-30 — Fireproof Men
    Lee, Robert G., *Bible Fires*. Grand Rapids: Zondervan Publishing House, 1956, p. 184.

27. *Fools*
    I Sam. 26:21-25 — Playing the Fool
    Ps. 53:1-3 — The Atheistic Fool
    Prov. 10:18 — The Slandering Fool
    Jer. 17:11 — The Dishonest Fool
    Matt. 25:1-13 — The Careless Fool
    Luke 12:13-21 — The Selfish Fool

28. *Funerals*
    Gen. 49:28 — 50:14 — The Burial of a Godly Father
    Deut. 34:1-8 — Buried by God
    II Kings 13:20, 21 — A Graveyard Miracle
    Mark 5:35-43 — A Death Without Burial

29. *Geographical Locations*
    Littorin, *How to Preach the Word with Variety*, pp. 104-107.
    Perry, *Manual for Biblical Preaching*, p. 118.
    Gen. 12:4-9 — Bethel, the House of God
    Num. 13:17-33 — Kadesh Barnea, a Holy Place
    Luke 2 and Ruth — Bethlehem, the House of Bread
    Luke 10:38-42 — Blessings at Bethany

30. *Historical Material* (Journeys & Historical Turning Points)

Broadus, *On the Preparation and Delivery of Sermons,* pp. 71, 72.
Burrell, *The Sermon: Its Content and Delivery,* pp. 87-95.
Dabney, *Sacred Rhetoric,* pp. 65-68.
Etter, *The Preacher and His Sermon,* p. 219.
Gibbs, *The Preacher and His Preaching,* pp. 252-256.
Littorin, *How to Preach the Word with Variety,* pp. 86-94.
Mark, *Patterns for Preaching,* pp. 168-172.
Perry, *Manual for Biblical Preaching,* pp. 114-116.
Porter, *Lectures on Homiletics and Preaching,* pp. 360-375.
Robbins, *Preaching the Gospel,* pp. 21-29.
   Num. 14:1-45 — Crisis at the Crossroads
   Josh. 3:14 — 4:18 — The Point of No Return
   Acts 16:6-10 — A Dream That Changed the World

31. *Hymns or Songs*
   Exod. 15:1-21 — A Song by the Sea
   Deut. 32:1-43 — The Song of Moses
   II Sam. 1:17-27 — A Song of Lamentation
   Rev. 5:6-10 — The Song of Redemption

32. *Interesting Incidents*
   Perry, *Manual for Biblical Preaching,* p. 111.
   I Sam. 6:1-16 — Confusing Cows
   I Sam. 10:17-27 — Hiding in the Stuff
   Matt. 26:47-56 — The Foolishness of Good Intentions
   John 8:1-11 — A Sermon in the Sand
   Acts 5:1-11 — Living a Lie
   Acts 19:11-20 — Strangers to the Evil Spirit

33. *Judgments*
   Isa. 29:1-16 — Judgment upon Deeds in the Dark
   Jer. 48:1-33 — The Glory Has Been Taken Away
   Rom. 2:1-16 — God's Verdict
   Rev. 20:11-15 — The Great White Throne

34. *Life Principles of Bible Characters* (See pp. 46–48.)
This life principle may be a direct statement of Scripture which forms the core for the major experiences of the individual or it may be wise to take the outstanding experiences of the character and formulate a phrase which could be the common denominator of the life.
   Perry, *Manual for Biblical Preaching,* p. 109.
   I Sam. 9-28 — Saul, a Man Who Played the Fool
   I Sam. 13-31 — Jonathan, a Man of Devotion
   Esther 1-10 — Esther, a Woman Who Counted the Cost

Acts 4, 9, 13-15 – Barnabas, a Man of Encouragement

35. *Marriages*
    Judg. 14:1-20 – A Mixed Marriage

36. *Men and Women of Prayer*
    Jonah 2:1-10 – Praying Under Pressure
    Eph. 1:15-23 – A Preacher Who Prayed for His People
    White, Reginald E. O., *They Teach Us to Pray*. New York: Harper and Brothers Publishers, 1957, p. 204.

37. *Miracles*
    Perry, *Manual for Biblical Preaching*, p. 128.
    I Kings 17:1-16 – Bread by the Brook
    II Kings 5:1-14 – Healing for the Hopeless
    John 9:1-41 – When Blind Eyes See
    Acts 3:1-11 – God's Wonder Working Ways

38. *Mountains*
    Gen. 22:1-14 – The Provision on the Mountain
    Matt. 17:1-13 – The Vision on the Mountain
    Macartney, Clarence Edward, *Mountains and Mountain Men of the Bible*. New York: Abingdon-Cokesbury Press, 1950, p. 188.

39. *Names of God*
    Gen. 22:14 – Jehovah Jireh: The Lord Who Provides
    Exod. 17:15 – Jehovah Nissi: The Lord Who Is a Banner
    Judg. 6:24 – Jehovah Shalom: The Lord Who Sends Peace
    Jer. 23:6 – Jehovah Tsidkenu: The Lord Who Is Our Righteousness
    Rolls, Charles J., *The Indescribable Christ*. Grand Rapids, Mich.: Zondervan Publishing House, 1953, p. 215.
    _____, *The World's Greatest Name*. Grand Rapids, Mich.: Zondervan Publishing House, 1956, p. 185.
    _____, *Time's Noblest Name*. Grand Rapids, Mich.: Zondervan Publishing House, 1958, p. 217.
    Stone, Nathan J., *Names of God in the Old Testament*. Chicago: Moody Press, 1944, p. 128.

40. *Night Scenes*
    Perry, *Manual for Biblical Preaching*, p. 131.
    Gen. 28:10-17 – A Night of Grace
    Gen. 32:22-32 – Wrestling in the Night
    Dan. 5:1-30 – Tragedy in the Night
    Dan. 6:1-28 – A Night Among Lions
    Matt. 2:1-10 – A Night to Remember

Luke 22:39-46 — Prayer in the Night
March, Rev. Daniel, *Night Scenes in the Bible.* Philadelphia: Zeigler and McCurdy, 1870, p. 544.
Wolston, W. T. P., *Night Scenes of Scripture.* Edinburgh: Gospel Messenger, 1899, p. 344.

41. *Parables*
    Jordan, *You Can Preach*, pp. 220-221.
    Littorin, *How to Preach the Word with Variety*, pp. 11-114.
    Perry, *Manual for Biblical Preaching*, p. 122.
    Robbins, *Preaching the Gospel*, pp. 51-59.
       Matt. 13:45, 46 — The Purchase of the Pearl
       Luke 8:4-18 — Seed, Soil, and Sower
       Luke 10:25-37 — Ambushed: A Tale of a Traveler
       Luke 14:15-24 — An Excuse or a Reason?
       Luke 15:1-32 — The Lost and Found Department
       Luke 19:11-27 — In Business for God
    Crowe, Charles M., *Sermons on the Parables of Jesus.* New York: Abingdon-Cokesbury Press, 1953, p. 186.
    Macartney, Clarence Edward, *The Parables of the Old Testament.* New York: Fleming H. Revell Co., 1916, p. 122.
    Morgan, G. Campbell, *The Parables and Metaphors of Our Lord.* Westwood, New Jersey: Fleming H. Revell Co., 1943, p. 352.

42. *Paradoxes*
    This is referred to by some as a dialecti or tension sermon.
    Mark, *Patterns for Preaching*, pp. 110-113.
    Jordan, *You Can Preach*, pp. 234-236.
       Mark 8:27—9:1 — Get God's Point of View
       II Cor. 4:16-18 — Seeing the Unseen
       II Cor. 12:1-10 — From Weakness to Strength
       Gal. 6:2, 5 — Who Will Carry the Burden?

43. *Periods of Bible History*
    Mark, *Patterns for Preaching*, pp. 148-152.
       Exod. 1-14 — The Egyptian Bondage: A Race of Slaves
       II Kings 23:36—25:30 — The Fall of a Nation

44. *Poetical Portions*
    Davis, *Design for Preaching*, pp. 55-57
       Ps. 1:1-6 — The Biography of the Blessed Life
       Ps. 32:1-11 — The Confession of a Saint

45. *Prayers*
    Littorin, *How to Preach the Word with Variety*, pp. 115-117.
    Perry, *Manual for Biblical Preaching*, p. 133.

II Sam. 7:18-29 – Praying to a Great God
II Kings 19:14-19 – Praying to Save a Nation
II Chron. 1:1-17 – A Wise Choice of a Wise Man
Hab. 3:1-19 – The Prayer of Faith
Matt. 6:6-13 – A Pattern for Prayer
John 17:1-26 – The Lord's Prayer
Bunzel, Claude, *Great Prayers of the Bible*. Pasadena, Calif.: Twentieth Century Evangelism, 1957, p. 133.
Chappell, Clovis G., *Sermons on the Lord's Prayer*. Nashville: Cokesbury Press, 1934, p. 221.
Kuiper, H. J., *Sermons of the Lord's Prayer*. Grand Rapids, Mich.: Zondervan Publishing House, 1956, p. 138.
Lockyer, Herbert, *All the Prayers of the Bible*. Grand Rapids, Mich.: Zondervan Publishing House, 1959, p. 281.
Macartney, Clarence Edward, *The Lord's Prayer*. New York: Fleming H. Revell Co., 1942, p. 87.
Pierce, Elinore Mapes, *The Prayers of the Bible*. Philadelphia: The Judson Press, 1944, p. 183.
Scroggie, W. Graham, *Paul's Prison Prayers*. London: Pickering & Inglis Ltd., 1921, p. 78.

46. *Prophetic Passages*
Ferris, *Go Tell the People*, pp. 35-38.
Perry, *Manual for Biblical Preaching*, pp. 134-135.
Littorin, *How to Preach the Word with Variety*, pp. 121-123.
Robbins, *Preaching the Gospel*, pp. 127-135.
Gen. 3:15 – A Ray of Hope in the Midst of Gloom
I Thess. 4:13-18 – God's Tomorrow, Today's Hope
Rev. 20 – The Thrilling Thousand Years

47. *Questions*
Jones, *Principles and Practice of Preaching*, pp. 103-104.
Gen. 3:8-24 – Where Are You?
Job 25:4 – How Can a Man Be Justified?
Ps. 42:3, 10 – Where Is Your God?
Matt. 12-12 – Which Is Worth More?
Matt. 16:13 – Who Am I?
John 21:15-19 – Do You Love Me?
Criswell, W. A., *Five Great Questions of the Bible*. Grand Rapids, Michigan: Zondervan, 1958, p. 55.
Macartney, Clarence Edward, *The Greatest Questions of the Bible and Life*. New York: Abingdon Press, 1948, p. 223.
Twelve Great Questions About Christ. Grand Rapids, Michigan: Baker Book House, 1956, p. 219.
Phillips, Harold Cooke, *Life's Unanswered Questions*. New York: Harper and Brothers, 1944, p. 170.

48. *Revivals*
   Perry, *Manual for Biblical Preaching*, p. 130.
   II Chron. 7:14 – A Formula for Revival
   II Chron. 29:1-11 – Revival Action
   II Chron. 34:1-33 – Reparation Brings Restoration
   Jonah 3 – Revival Preaching
   Autrey, C. E., *Revivals of the Old Testament*. Grand Rapids, Michigan: Zondervan Publishing House, 1960, p. 155.

49. *Romances*
   Gen. 29 – Romance and Deceit
   Ruth 2-4 – The Romances of a Woman of Worth
   Faulkner, James, *Romances and Intrigues of the Woman of the Bible*. New York: Vantage Press, 1957, p. 162.

50. *Sermons*
   Perry, *Manual for Biblical Preaching*, p. 120.
   Acts 2:14-36 – Pentecostal Preaching
   Acts 13:16-41 – A Christ-Centered Sermon
   Josh. 24:1-15 – Your Day of Decision
   I Sam. 12:1-18 – The Eloquence of Godliness

51. *Spies*
   Num. 13:1–14:45 – Mission Impossible
   Judge. 7:9-14 – Spying on a Dream
   II Kings 6:8-19 – An Army of the Blind
   Matt. 26:47-56 – The Kiss of the Spy

52. *Theophanies*
   Perry, *Manual for Biblical Preaching*, p. 132.
   Gen. 16:7-14 – An Angel by a Spring
   Exod. 24:1-11 – Standing on Sapphire Stone
   Exod. 33:1-23 – Seeing Eye to Eye
   Dan. 3:24-30 – The Fourth Man

53. *Trees*
   Ps. 92:12 – Palmtree Christians
   Gal. 3:10-14 – The Curse of Hanging on a Tree

54. *Trials of Great Men and Women*
   Ruth 1:1-5 – Lost! A Husband and Two Sons
   Job 23:10 – I Shall Come Forth as Gold
   Macartney, Clarence Edward, *Trials of Great Men of the Bible*. New York: Abingdon-Cokesbury Press, 1946, p. 189.

55. *Types* (See p. 43–44.)
   Mark, *Patterns for Preaching*, pp. 35-40.
   Perry, *Manual for Biblical Preaching*, p. 124.

Gen. 6:14, I Peter 3:20, 21 — The Ark, a Type of Christ
Gen. 14:18, Hebrews 7:1-17 — Melchizedek, a Type of Christ

56. *Visions*
Ezek. 37:1-14 — Dry Bones in the Valley
Acts 26:19-23 — The Heavenly Vision
Rev. 1:9-20 — A Vision of His Glory

C. By Using Different-Sized Portions of the Bible

Book of the Bible Sermon
Blackwood, *Preaching from the Bible*, pp. 169-181.
Caemmerer, *Preaching for the Church*, pp. 150-161.
Jones, *Principles and Practices of Preaching*, pp. 109-110.
Perry, *Manual for Biblical Preaching*, p. 126.
Whitesell & Perry, *Variety in Your Preaching*, pp. 41-43.
Sermon Suggestions
Jonah — God Employs Frail Witnesses
Ruth — Triumphant Faith
Esther — The Protection of Providence
Hag. — A Display of God's Greatness
Gal. — Justification By Faith
Heb. — Better Things
James — Practical Christianity
Philem. — Writing a Christian Letter
I John — This We Know

Chapter of the Bible Sermon
Blackwood, *Preaching from the Bible*, pp. 135-142.
Jones, *Principles and Practice of Preaching*, p. 109.
Mark, *Patterns for Preaching*, pp. 160-165.
Whitesell & Perry, *Variety in Your Preaching*, pp. 39, 40.
Sermon Suggestions
Ps. 19 — How God Speaks
Ps. 23 — Saviour and Shepherd
Isa. 53 — The Gospel According to Isaiah
Isa. 55 — Satisfaction Guaranteed
Rom. 8 — More Than Conquerors
Heb. 11 — Faith in Action
II Peter 3:1-18 — How to Live in the Atomic Age
Rev. 22:1-21 — God's Last Word to Man

Paragraph of the Bible Sermon, Combinational Sermon, or Section Sermon
Blackwood, *Preaching from the Bible*, pp. 94-110.

Littorin, *How to Preach the Word with Variety*, pp. 51-54.
Mark, *Patterns for Preaching*, pp. 124-129, 165-168.
Whitesell & Perry, *Variety in Your Preaching*, pp. 37-39.
Sermon Suggestions
Josh. 1:1-9 — Secrets of Success
Ps. 3-5 — Hounded But Happy
Prov. 30:24-28 — Four Midgets As Teachers
Mark 5:1-20 — When Jesus Comes
II Tim. 4:6-8 — The Satisfaction of a Godly Life
Phil. 4:4-7 — A Prescription for Peace
I Peter 5:1-11 — Precious Promises

Verse of the Bible Sermon
Blackwood, *The Preparation of Sermons*, pp. 55-63.
Broadus, *A Treatise on the Preparation and Delivery of Sermons*, pp. 293-298.
Caldwell, *Preaching Angles*, pp. 28-48.
Dabney, *Sacred Rhetoric*, pp. 218-220.
Hoyt, *The Work of Preaching*, pp. 175-179.
Kidder, *A Treatise on Homiletics*, pp. 201-206.
Ripley, *Sacred Rhetoric*, pp. 109-120.
Shedd, *Homiletics and Pastoral Theology*, pp. 149-153.
Sermon Suggestions
I Tim. 3:16 — The Mystery of Godliness
Ps. 34:4 — God Hears
Luke 9:33 — The Demands of Discipleship
I Peter 3:18 — The Cost of Freedom

Key Word or *Key Phrase of the Bible Sermon*
Caldwell, *Preaching Angles*, pp. 30-32.
Mark, *Patterns for Preaching*, pp. 22-26, 74-78, 172-178.
Perry, *Manual for Biblical Preaching*, pp. 87-89.
Sermon Suggestions
"Better" — 11 times in Hebrews
"In the Heavenlies" — 5 times in Ephesians
"Lamb" — 28 times in Revelation
"Straightway" — 42 times in Mark

D. By Using a Starting Sermon Idea from an Extra-Biblical Source

The types of sermons noted in this section represent areas in which the sermonizer may find a seed thought which, with proper nourishment, may develop into a Biblical sermon. Although the idea has its genesis outside the Scriptures, its truth must correspond to Biblical truth. Unless the idea and its development can be supported from

Variation of the Outline 81

the Scripture, it should not be used. These types of sermons will be strengthened by the use of visual aids. Because of the uniqueness of their content, they are helpful in meeting the challenges offered by special occasions.

The preacher must be careful lest he becomes so enthralled with the unique source of his preaching idea that he forgets that his primary task is to use this only as a vehicle for effectively presenting Biblical truth.

There are suggestions which can be given as possible sermonic processes available for use with these rather unique types of sermons. In some cases, the content of the material in the extra-Biblical source will force the sermonizer to use other than the process suggested.

I. *Modification Process:* There are *nine* of these sermons which will normally employ the modification process:
   1. Christian Classic Sermon
   2. Dramatic Book Sermon
   3. Church History Sermon
   4. Denominational Sermon
   5. Great Life Sermon
   6. Music or Hymn Sermon
   7. Great Painting Sermon
   8. Great Poem Sermon
   9. Testimony Sermon

   A. The *subject* is obtained from the extra-Biblical source. It must be a subject however which is in agreement with the teaching of Scripture.
   B. The *theme* is an aspect of the subject as emphasized in the extra-Biblical source.
   C. The *proposition* is the theme in sentence form.
   D. The *transitional sentence* has no unique features except for the fact that it does not conclude with Scripture. (See pp. 58–60.) In place of the Scripture reference, there is reference to the particular extra-Biblical source which provides the idea for the sermon.
   E. The *main points* have their source in an aspect of the extra-Biblical area. The main points correspond to a key word just as in any modification sermon. The truth set forth in each main point must be shown to be in accord with the teaching of a specific passage of Scripture or to be in accord with the general teaching and emphasis of Scripture.

Sermon Type	Possible Sources of Points
1. *Christian Classic Sermon*	Chapters of the classic
	Characters within the classic
	Outstanding events
2. *Dramatic Book Sermon*	(Same as above)
3. *Church History Sermon*	Periods within the historical segment
	Outstanding characters

		Outstanding events
4.	*Denominational Sermon*	Affirmations in the creed
		Items of polity
5.	*Great Life Sermon*	Outstanding events
		Points of crisis
6.	*Music or Hymn Sermon*	Stanzas of the hymn
7.	*Great Painting Sermon*	Characters within the painting
		Items within the painting
		Unique features of the painting
8.	*Great Poem Sermon*	Verses of the Poem
9.	*Testimony Sermon*	Outstanding events in a life

  F. *Subpoints* should be obtained from the extra-Biblical source if possible.

  G. The *conclusion* has no unique features.

  H. The *introduction* deals with the extra-Biblical source as that source is or can be related to the listeners. The *explanation* discusses the unique features of this type of sermon and shows the relationship between the extra-Biblical source and the testimony of Scripture.

II. *Clarification Process:*

  Quotation or Slogan Sermon: Sermon Type 4, pp. 46–48
  Astronomy Sermon: Sermon Type 1, pp. 43–44
  Object or Hobby Sermon: Sermon Type 1, pp. 43–44
  Modern Parable Sermon: Sermon Type 1, pp. 43–44

Astronomy Sermon (See Sermon Type 1, pp. 43–44.)

  Luccock, *In the Minister's Workshop*, pp. 134-147.

  Broadus, *On the Preparation and Delivery of Sermons*, pp. 200, 287, 288.

  Pattison, *Making the Sermon*, pp. 278-280.

  Phelps, *Theory of Preaching*, pp. 154, 155.

   Ps. 19:1 – The Sermon in the Sky

   Ps. 84:11 – The Lamp of Heaven

   Mal. 4:2 – The Sun of Righteousness

   Rev. 22:16 – The Bright and Morning Star

Christian Classic Sermon (Possible Sources)

  Bunyan, John, *Pilgrim's Progress*. New York: Holt, Rinehart & Winston, 1961, p. 338.

  Brother Laurence, *The Practice of the Presence of God*. Old Tappan, New Jersey: Fleming H. Revell.

  McConkey, James H., *The Three-Fold Secret of the Holy Spirit*. Harrisburg, Pa.: James H. McConkey, 1897, p. 123.

Church History Sermon

  Blackwood, *Planning a Year's Pulpit Work*, pp. 171-184.

  Broadus, *On the Preparation and Delivery of Sermons*, pp. 71-73.

Etter, *The Preacher and His Sermon*, pp. 92, 93.
Hoppin, *Homiletics*, pp. 404, 405.
The Reformation Period emphasized the need of a man who would protest against corruption, reaffirm Biblical Christianity, and live the truth he believed.

Denominational Sermon
An individual sermon or a series of sermons may be preached on denominational distinctives. Emphasis should be placed upon their Biblical foundation.

Dramatic Book Sermon (Possible Sources)
Dostoveski, Fedor M., *Crime and Punishment*. Trans. Constance Garnett. New York: Modern Library of Random House, Inc., 1950, p. 532. Sin and its consequences is stressed.

Eliot, George, *Ramola*. New York: Everyman's Library of E. D. Dutton & Company, Inc. Sin and Retribution is stressed.

Hawthorne, Nathaniel, *The Scarlet Letter*. New York: Modern Library of Random House, Inc. Sin and conscience is stressed.

Tolstoy, Leo N., *The Resurrection*. New York: Washington Square Press of Simon & Schuster. Conversion is stressed.

Great Life Sermon
These four books provide a short account of the lives of many great men and women and relate the life to a verse of Scripture which had special significance for them.

Boreham, Frank W., *A Bunch of Everlastings*. Philadelphia: Judson Press, 1949, p. 256.

_____, *A Casket of Cameos*. Philadelphia: Judson Press, 1950, p. 271.

_____, *A Faggot of Torches*. Philadelphia: Judson Press, 1951, p. 268.

_____, *A Handful of Stars*. Philadelphia: Judson Press, 1950, p. 261.

Modern Parable Sermon (See Sermon Type 1, pp. 43-44.)
The account of an experience in the life of the preacher or of one within the scope of his reading in the news can provide a modern illustration for teaching Biblical truth.

Music Sermon
In some cases a series of messages can grow out of one hymn. The sermonizer should find a Biblical passage or passages which aptly express, reinforce, and elaborate the basic truth of the hymn. The message should be kept in accord with the mood of the hymn.

Caldwell, *Preaching Angles*, pp. 84-89.
Caemmerer, *Preaching for the Church*, p. 174.

Stidger, *Preaching Out of the Overflow,* pp. 116-119.
"Great is Thy Faithfulness" — Lam. 3:22, 23.
"A Mighty Fortress is Our God" — Ps. 46, Eph. 6:11-13, Revelation 19:11-16, I John 5:4, 5.
"Beneath the Cross" — The Shadow of the Cross.
"There is a Green Hill" — The Simplicity of the Cross.
"When I Survey" — The Wonder of the Cross.
"O Sacred Head Now Wounded"—The Mystery of the Cross.
"Come, Holy Spirit" — The Power of the Holy Spirit.
"What a Friend" — Benefits of His Friendship.
"In the Cross of Christ I Glory"—The Greatness of His Cross.
"I Need Thee Every Hour" — The Blessings of His Presence.
McCutchan, R. C., *Hymns in the Lives of Men.* New York: Abingdon-Cokesbury, 1945.
Hart, William J., *Hymn Stories of the 20th Century.* Boston: W. A. Wilde Co., 1948.

Object or Hobby Sermon (See Sermon Type 1, pp. 43-44.)

This sermon presents divine truth by means of objects. This may involve the use of an object employed by Scripture (Genesis 9:12-17) or an object suggested by a text (Isaiah 64:6).

A Coin Collector:	Luke 20:24 — Faces on Coins
	Matt. 17:27 — Coins and Fish
	Matt. 25:18 — Hidden Treasure
A Fisherman:	Matt. 17:27 — Fish as Tribute
	Matt. 4:19 — Fisherman
	Amos 4:2 — Fishhooks
A Star Gazer:	Josh. 10:13 — Sun and Moon Stood Still
	Gen. 1:16 — Origin of Stars
	Ps. 147:4 — Counting Stars
	Rev. 22:16 — Bright and Morning Star

Great Painting Sermon (See p. 65.)
Caldwell, *Preaching Angles,* pp. 81-83.
Sollitt, *Preaching from Pictures.*
"The Light of the World" by Hunt
"Christ and the Doctors" by Hofmann
"Christ and the Fisherman" by Zimmermann
"Christ and the Rich Young Ruler" by Hofmann
"The Last Supper" by DaVinci
"Christ Before Pilate" by Munkacsy
"Come Unto Me" by Block
Maus, Cynthia P., *Christ and the Fine Arts.* New York: Harper & Brothers Publishers, 1938, p. 764.
Bailey, Albert E., *The Gospel in Art.* Philadelphia: United Church Press, 1944.

Branch, Harold Francis, *Christ's Ministry and Passion in Art.* Philadelphia: H. M. Shelley, 1929.
—————————, *Sermons on Great Paintings.* Philadelphia: H. M. Shelley, 1930.
—————————, *Religious Picture Sermons.* Philadelphia: H. M. Shelley, 1934.
Carter, James R., *The Gospel Message in Great Pictures.* New York: Funk and Wagnalls, 1929.
Cavert, W. D., *Story Sermons from Literature and Art.* New York: Harper & Brothers Publishers, 1939.
Pace, C. N., *Pictures That Preach.* New York: Abingdon Press, 1924.

Great Poem Sermon
This sermon uses poetry in a determinative relation to the basic message of the sermon. The parts of the poem may provide main divisions for the sermon.
Caldwell, *Preaching Angles,* pp. 89-96.
"Live Christ" by John Oxenham
"Prayer, What is It?" by Robert Maguire
"The Mustard Seed" by Robert Maguire
"You, An Answer to Prayer" by A. D. Burkett
"And Christ is Crucified Anew" by John Moreland
Kerr, Hugh T., *The Gospel in Modern Poetry.* New York: Fleming H. Revell, 1926, p. 187.
Stidger, William L., *Flames of Faith.* New York: The Abingdon Press, 1922, p. 204.
Stidger, William L., *Giant Hours with Poet Preachers.* New York: The Abingdon Press, 1918, p. 127.

Quotation or Slogan Sermon (See Sermon Type 4, pp. 46–48.)
"Stand Firm." — Duke of Wellington at Waterloo
"If I had a thousand heads I would lose them all rather than recant." — Martin Luther
"I only regret that I have but one life to give for my country." — Nathan Hale

Testimony Sermon
This sermon tells of one's own personal experience of God's saving grace. It is recommended that such a sermon have a Biblical basis. Acts 9 suggests that conversion involves a choice, change, and challenge.
Gibbs, *The Preacher and His Preaching,* pp. 208-217.

E. By Placing Special Emphasis Upon the Purpose of the Sermon

1. *Apologetic Sermon*

This sermon is a reply to attacks made on the Christian faith.
McCracken, *The Making of the Sermon*, pp. 48-50.
Sangster, *The Craft of the Sermon*, pp. 45-48.
Wood, *The Preacher's Workshop*, pp. 54-57.

2. *Argumentative Sermon*
   This sermon aims either to convince one whom from unbelief, doubt, or disbelief does not accept a given truth, or to confirm in his belief one who does accept it. The position to be maintained should be given in the proposition. The syllogism is the framework of this sermon and belief is the desired result.
   Fisk, *Manual of Preaching*, pp. 226-231.
   Phelps, *The Theory of Preaching*, p. 35.

3. *Classification Sermon* or *Categorizing Sermon*
   This sermon divides people and things into different classes and types. It breaks the material of the sermon into various categories.
   Jones, *Principles and Practice of Preaching*, p. 105.
   Luccock, *In the Minister's Workshop*, pp. 138-140.
   Sangster, *The Craft of the Sermon*, pp. 92-99.

4. *Commentary Sermon*
   This sermon uses the experience of people to provide concrete examples of the validity of the truth of the text.
   Mark, *Patterns for Preaching*, pp. 136-139.

5. *Corrective Sermon* or *Rebuttal Sermon*
   This sermon is designed to correct some error or false teaching. This may pertain to doctrine or duty. Each false teaching would form the basis of a main point of the message. The refutation of the error would be in the subdivisions.
   Jones, *Principles and Practice of Preaching*, p. 107.
   Luccock, *In the Minister's Workshop*, pp. 145-146.
   Mark, *Patterns for Preaching*, pp. 131-136.

6. *Doctrinal Sermon* or *Theological Sermon*
   This sermon sets forth the distinctive truths of revelation for the edification of the hearers. This may be presented didactically, polemically, or apologetically.
   Brastow, *Work of the Preacher*, pp. 171-201.
   Breed, *Preparing to Preach*, pp. 427-446.
   Broadus, *On the Preparation and Delivery of Sermons*, pp. 59-66.
   Burrell, *The Sermon: Its Construction and Delivery*, pp. 81-86.
   Dabney, *Sacred Rhetoric*, pp. 50-56.
   Fritz, *Essentials of Preaching*, pp. 46-53.

Johnson, *The Ideal Ministry*, pp. 177-183, 361-363.
Jordan, *You Can Preach*, pp. 223-227.
Kidder, *A Treatise on Homiletics*, pp. 274, 275.
Mark, *Patterns for Preaching*, pp. 40-44.
McCracken, *The Making of the Sermon*, pp. 45-47.
Montgomery, *Preparing Preachers to Preach*, pp. 137-140.
Porter, *Lectures on Homiletics and Preaching*, pp. 323-333.
Skinner, *Aids to Revealing and Hearing*, pp. 107-157.
Wood, *The Preacher's Workshop*, pp. 50-53.

7. *Ethical Sermon*
This sermon gives instruction in the moral laws which govern social and industrial life. It is aimed at the building up of Christian character. It aims at the enforcement of some Christian duty, or at the securing of the practice of some Christian obligation or privilege.
Blackwood, *The Preparation of Sermons*, pp. 31-34.
Brastow, *Work of the Preacher*, pp. 202-229.
Dabney, *Sacred Rhetoric*, pp. 56-64.
Hoyt, *The Preacher: His Person, Message and Method*, pp. 326-345.
Johnson, *The Ideal Ministry*, pp. 363-365.
Kidder, *A Treatise on Homiletics*, pp. 276, 277.
Porter, *Lectures on Homiletics and Preaching*, pp. 346-359.
Robbins, *Preaching the Gospel*, pp. 94-101.
Sangster, *The Craft of the Sermon*, pp. 39-42.

8. *Evangelistic Sermon* or *Soul Winning Sermon*
This sermon is one which seeks to promote conviction of sin and to lead men to an immediate decision for Jesus Christ. It aims to bring men to a confession of faith.
Brastow, *Work of the Preacher*, pp. 230-257.
Breed, *Preparing to Preach*, pp. 401-413.
Davis, *Design for Preaching*, pp. 138-160.
Graves, *Lectures on Homiletics*, pp. 125-134.
Hoyt, *The Preacher: His Person, Message and Method*, pp. 261-263.
Johnson, *The Ideal Ministry*, pp. 477-489.
Jordan, *You Can Preach*, pp. 242-252.
Kern, *The Ministry to the Congregation*, pp. 441-454.
McCracken, *The Making of the Sermon*, pp. 60, 61.
Moore, *Preacher's Problems*, pp. 352-369.
Riley, *Preacher and His Preaching*, pp. 86-93.
Sangster, *The Craft of the Sermon*, pp. 53-61.
Weatherspoon, *Sent Forth to Preach*, pp. 102-126.

9. *Expansive Sermon* or *Observational Sermon*
   This sermon provides added truth so that the text, which at first might have appeared to be untrue or the statement of only a partial truth is expanded. This expansion comes through the application of sanctified imagination and common sense to an historical event.
   Mark, *Patterns for Preaching*, pp. 89-92, 139-142.
   Montgomery, *Preparing Preachers to Preach*, pp. 134-136.

10. *Experiential Sermon*
    This sermon aims at stimulating spiritual growth.
    Etter, *The Preacher and His Sermon*, pp. 221-224.
    Perry, *Manual for Biblical Preaching*, p. 127.

11. *Expository Sermon*
    This sermon aims to instruct the hearer by unfolding to him the meaning of a connected portion of Scripture. The portion may consist of a few or many verses which have a central thought or theme. It involves the explanation of a passage and the application of its truth.
    Breed, *Preparing to Preach*, pp. 387-398
    Evans, *How to Prepare Sermons and Chapel Addresses*, pp. 111-115.
    Fisk, *Manual of Preaching*, pp. 201-205.
    Gibbs, *The Preacher and His Preaching*, pp. 218-236.
    Hogg, *A Handbook of Homiletics and Practical Theology*, pp. 47-49.
    Hoppin, *Homiletics*, pp. 447-449.
    Kidder, *A Treatise on Homiletics*, pp. 268-271.
    Littorin, *How to Preach the Word with Variety*, pp. 27-43.
    McCracken, *The Making of the Sermon*, pp. 78-82.
    Riley, *Preacher and His Preaching*, pp. 76-77.
    Shedd, *Homiletics and Pastoral Theology*, pp. 153-158.
    Whitesell, *The Art of Biblical Preaching*, pp. 51-56.
    Whitesell & Perry, *Variety in Your Preaching*, pp. 34-36.
    Wood, *The Preacher's Workshop*, pp. 35-41.

12. *Life Situation Sermon* (See p. 51.)
    This sermon starts with a real-life issue or problem and deals with it honestly. It seeks to provide a Biblical solution to the problem. It originates in the experience of the people to whom it is preached with the specific aim of bringing help to their situation.
    Caldwell, *Preaching Angles*, pp. 108-113.
    Jordan, *You Can Preach*, pp. 218-220.

Kemp, *Life Situation Preaching,* p. 24.
Luccock, *In the Minister's Workshop,* pp. 50-92.
Mark, *Patterns for Preaching,* pp. 117-120.
McCracken, *The Making of the Sermon,* pp. 62, 63.
Sangster, *The Craft of the Sermon,* pp. 129, 130.

13. *Narrative Sermon*
    This sermon conveys instruction by means of example. It provides a unified series of events in which persons and happenings interact to produce a crisis and outcome. It is a story sermon. The outcome depends upon the crisis and the forces that produced it.
    Breed, *Preparing to Preach,* pp. 375-384.
    Davis, *Design for Preaching,* pp. 180, 181.
    Jones, *Principles and Practice of Preaching,* pp. 113, 114.

14. *Orientation Sermon*
    This sermon helps the hearers differentiate between the vital and the unimportant.
    Jordan, *You Can Preach,* pp. 230, 231.

15. *Persuasive Sermon*
    This sermon has as its primary objective the moving of the will.
    Fisk, *Manual of Preaching,* pp. 237-243.

16. *Social Sermon* (See p. 51.)
    This sermon is one which combats social evils.
    McCracken, *The Making of the Sermon,* pp. 51-55.
    Sangster, *The Craft of the Sermon,* pp. 48-53.
    Wood, *The Preacher's Workshop,* pp. 48, 49.

17. *Spiritualizing Sermon*
    This sermon gives an exposition of a passage followed by the drawing of a spiritual lesson.
    Littorin, *How to Preach the Word with Variety,* pp. 55-63.

18. *Topical Sermon* or *Thematic Sermon* or *Selective Sermon*
    This is a sermon occupied with one subject. The subject may be drawn from a text but it is discussed independently of the text. In this type of sermon, the subject is normally divided according to its nature.
    Blackwood, *The Preparation of Sermons,* pp. 101-108.
    Broadus, *On the Preparation and Delivery of Sermons,* pp. 288-292.
    Etter, *The Preacher and His Sermon,* pp. 180-183.
    Gibbs, *The Preacher and His Preaching,* pp. 224-251.
    Hogg, *A Handbook of Homiletics and Pastoral Theology,* pp. 41-43.

Kidder, *A Treatise on Homiletics*, pp. 206-214.
Littorin, *How to Preach the Word with Variety*, pp. 64-67, 79-85.
Riley, *Preacher and His Preaching*, pp. 72, 73.
Shedd, *Homiletics and Pastoral Theology*, pp. 144-149.
Whitesell, *The Art of Biblical Preaching*, pp. 44-47.
Whitesell & Perry, *Variety in Your Preaching*, pp. 40, 41.

F. By Varying the Items within the Sermon Outline Proposition

It is important that the substance of the proposition be recognized and clearly understood by the listener. The preacher should repeat it until he is certain that it has been grasped by the listener. This repetition may become monotonous unless the form of the proposition is varied.

The declarative form
"Prayer brings many benefits."
The interrogative form
"What are the benefits of prayer?"
The hortatory form
"Keep on seeking the benefits of prayer!"
The exclamatory form
"Think of the many benefits of prayer."

The method of introducing the proposition may be varied by using one of the following phrases.

I invite your attention . . .
The text contains . . .
This discourse will be devoted to . . .
I propose to speak . . .
I aim to prove . . .
My intention is to illustrate . . .
The text is an example of . . .
The service of this hour will consider . . .
Let us consider this truth . . .
Our common experience emphasizes . . .

In the sermon outline the proposition appears just following the introduction. In normal presentation it is delivered at this same point in the sermon. There are times, however, when the place of presentation of the proposition can be varied. The main points of the sermon can be presented and then the proposition delivered which will then serve to provide a unifying thought climax to the sermon. This is the difference between deductive and inductive sermon presentation.

Main Divisions

The type of sermon and the key word selected will provide variety for the main points of a message. There are three additional suggestions.

The main divisions may be formulated so that they provide the basis for an acrostic.

F — Fun	Words	Ps. 19:14	Jesus
A — Altar	Actions	I Thess. 5:6	Others
M — Master	Thoughts	Ps. 19:14	Yourself
I — Instruction	Company	Ps. 1:1	
L — Love	Heart	Prov. 4:23	
Y — Yardstick			

When the main divisions have been formulated according to either the modification or clarification sermon process, they may then be surveyed for alliterative possibilities. This means that each main division will have as its core a word beginning with the same sound as the core words in the other main divisions. Alliteration must never be sought at the expense of logic.

Alan Monroe of Purdue University in his book, *Principles and Types of Speech*, developed what he termed the motivated sequence. If this were used as a sermon outline, there would be five steps. There would be no introduction, proposition, or conclusion, as such. This is a psychological approach to a speech outline. There would be five main divisions.

The attention step (Making the audience wish to listen)
The need step (Creating the idea that this is the thing to do, believe or satisfy the need)
The satisfaction step (Getting the audience to agree that your proposal is correct)
The visualization step (Causing the listener to picture himself enjoying the satisfaction of doing, believing, or feeling this action)
The action step (Asking the listener to do, believe, or feel what we present)

Introduction

The preacher may select one or more purposes from the following list and thereby vary the content of the introduction:

To establish contact with the audience
To arouse interest in the text or theme being discussed by emphasizing its importance and clarifying the terms
To remove prejudice against the speaker or his subject
To show the pertinence of the theme to the occasion

To bring calmness to the audience

To enlighten the listeners regarding the background of the message

To point out the necessity for finding a solution to a particular problem

To clarify the unique features of form and content which the sermon will possess

There are many instruments or materials which the sermonizer can employ within the introduction.

(1) A startling statement
(2) A challenging question or series of questions
(3) A pertinent quotation
(4) A witty, humorous, or amusing incident
(5) An epigram (a bright or witty thought tersely and ingeniously expressed)
(6) A vivid word picture
(7) A definition
(8) A comparison
(9) A discovery
(10) A correction
(11) A concession
(12) A paradox
(13) A rhetorical question (a question not intended to elicit an answer but inserted for rhetorical effect)
(14) A statement of a problem
(15) A reference to a cartoon
(16) An object lesson (if speaking to a "believing audience")
(17) An announcement of something significant
(18) A proposal
(19) A personal observation
(20) A commendation
(21) A statement of the special importance of the theme
(22) A conundrum (a puzzling question of which the answer is a pun or involves a pun) or riddle
(23) A prediction or prophecy
(24) A brief poem
(25) A brief history of the theme
(26) A proverb
(27) A prayer
(28) A pertinent, courteous reference to a previous speaker
(29) A gracious acknowledgment of the speaker's introduction
(30) A reference to a popular book
(31) A reference to a current event
(32) An incident from pastoral experience
(33) A reference to a special season
(34) A sentence from a book widely read
(35) A comparison with other Scripture passages
(36) A dramatic description

Conclusion

There are at least five different types of conclusions. The sermonizer may select from this list and thereby increase the element of variety.

The recapitulation or summary conclusion restates the main points of the message. They may be restated exactly as given or paraphrased. There are some instances where the point can be summarized by one word. This process would provide an epigrammatic summary.

The application made under each main point may be summarized. This will emphasize the ways and means of applying the main divisions of the message to the daily life of the listeners.

One or more of the basic appeals may be stressed. This will be one way of providing a motivation to the listener to accept the truth of the message. Dr. Charles Koller in his book, *Expository Preaching Without Notes*, lists these basic appeals as altruism, aspiration, curiosity, duty, fear, love, and reason.

When the main thrust of the message has been negative, the sermonizer will find it profitable to use a contrast conclusion thus ending his message on a positive note.

If the preacher feels that his listeners will have objections in their minds which will prompt them to refrain from accepting or acting upon his message, he may list and meet these anticipated objections in the conclusion.

The speaker may select one or more of the instruments listed below to enhance the effectiveness of the conclusion.

(1) A restatement of the text
(2) An apt quotation
(3) A fitting poem
(4) An earnest exhortation
(5) A story or illustration
(6) An appeal to the imagination
(7) A contrasting truth
(8) A prayer
(9) An answer to objections
(10) A call for public response
(11) A rhetorical question
(12) An appreciation
(13) A proverb
(14) A promise
(15) A suggestion of ways and means
(16) A striking statement
(17) A parable
(18) A hymn

The changing of the mood in presentation will provide a useful means for gaining variety. The nature of the sermon, type of content, and occasion will provide guidance in the selection of a mood.

The quiet mood
The mood of overwhelming appeal
The comforting mood
The contemplative mood
The bright and joyful mood
The worshipful or devotional mood

Illustrations

The preacher should select the illustrations for his sermon from a variety of sources. He should beware of having too many from personal experience and too few from the Bible. A starting list of some of these sources would include:

(1) Bible
(2) Personal observation
(3) Personal experience
(4) Children
(5) Literature
(6) Hymns
(7) Novels
(8) Art
(9) Electronic media
(10) Imagination
(11) Traditional illustrations
(12) History
(13) Missions
(14) Comparative religions
(15) Nature
(16) Athletics
(17) Science
(18) Travel
(19) Hobbies

Some of the more common types of illustrations which may be gleaned from the sources listed above include:

(1) Stories
(2) Parables
(3) Allegories
(4) Myths
(5) Object lessons
(6) Anecdotes
(7) Dramatics
(8) Poems
(9) Proverbs
(10) Quotations
(11) Figures of speech
(12) Analogies

The speaker should vary his techniques in using illustrations. He will normally have one major illustration for each main point. The type of sermon may be one factor which will prompt him to alter the number of illustrations. Biographical, parabolic, and historical messages do not need as many illustrations as do doctrinal messages. Extremely long illustrations should seldom be used. The point of the illustration does not always have to be specifically stated. If it is a good illustration, the point should be obvious. It is wise to vary the age appeal of illustrations. There should be something for all age groups within the congregation. It is not always needful or wise to introduce each illustration in a formal fashion.

IV

PRESENTATION OF THE BIBLICAL SERMON

IV. PRESENTATION OF THE BIBLICAL SERMON

A. Plan Your Preaching for the Special Days and Seasons

It is profitable for the preacher to plan a preaching program. One of the best times to prepare such a program is during the vacation period. The preacher can reflect upon the program of the past and then make some projections for the months ahead. The aim is to provide a general timesaving guide for the preacher which will serve his particular needs. It should not be considered as an arrangement which cannot be changed as conditions dictate.

This type of plan will not only save time, but will encourage the preacher to make better use of his time. It will encourage the preacher to collect helpful books in advance and survey their contents. It will help the church musicians in that they will be able to plan music which will provide support for the messages. It will help the sermonizer avoid an overlapping of subject matter and at the same time make certain that his people are being exposed to the various types of content within the Scriptures.

Several books are available to help the preacher in his planning.

> Blackwood, Andrew W., *Planning a Year's Pulpit Work*. New York: Abingdon Press, 1942, p. 240.
>
> Gibson, George Miles, *Planned Preaching*. Philadelphia: The Westminster Press, 1954, p. 140.
>
> Pearce, J. Winston, *Planning Your Preaching*. Nashville, Tennessee: Broadman Press, 1967, p. 197.

In the process of determining the special times to be observed and those to be omitted during the year, it will be wise to check the outline of the Christian year, the civil calendar, the particular church history and customs of the particular church, and the denominational planbook.

The special occasion for the sermon will have an effect upon the sermon. It will be a controlling factor in the choice of materials, the form of the outline to be used, and the goal for the sermon. The background of the occasion and the surrounding events and personalities may provide illustrative material. The introduction of the message may be built around an incident in the history of the occasion, a personality connected with it, or a current problem or event that has bearing upon the occasion.

In the presentation of the special occasion message, the speaker should give consideration to the place which the message should have within the total program. He must be prepared to adapt himself to the special circumstances of that particular service. Sudden sobering circumstances may arise or unforeseen distractions may appear. He must have his message so firmly in mind that he can adjust his manner to the occasion without losing his grasp of the sermon.

Visual aids can often be used with profit in support of the special occasion message. They should aid the message and not be a substitute for it. Careful timing and planning should be arranged. If objects are used, they should be related to the theme of the entire message.

The clothes worn by the speaker should be appropriate for the occasion. They should not draw attention to the speaker. He will want to arrive ahead of time in order to check the final arrangements and to accustom himself to the atmosphere of the occasion. He should know the length of time which he is expected to speak and should stay within that limit.

Since special occasion preaching offers some unique challenges, it will be wise to make certain that one checks the following items.

1. Do you know the background and present status of the group comprising the audience?
2. Have you selected illustrations which will have interest and meaning for that particular audience?
3. Is there an object or other visual aid which it would be appropriate and practical for you to use?
4. Have you shown sincere respect for this group by preparing a message with it in mind rather than just repeating a message which was written for some other group?
5. Can you summarize your message in a succinct statement which the listeners can carry away with them?
6. Is your message geared to meet a need in the lives of the anticipated listeners?
7. Have you checked the age and educational level of the anticipated listeners?
8. Are you well enough prepared so that you can speak without notes?
9. Are you aware of the time limits for your message?
10. Do you know of any special biases which your listeners may have regarding the subject on which you are to speak?
11. Have you taken the fact into consideration that there will probably be people with differing amounts of Bible information in their backgrounds?

PRESENTATION

12. Would it be practical to have some audience participation involved in your presentation?
13. Have you made preparation within your message for the fact that the attention span of most listeners is more limited than we think?
14. Have you incorporated some relevant humor within your message?
15. Have you remembered that there may be those present at this special occasion for whom this will be one of the few times when they will hear the message of Jesus Christ?

The presentation of the message will be more effective if you as speaker make provision for the following:

1. If you are arranging the program, be sure that there is not so much special music that the message is made ineffective.
2. Adjust your formality or informality to the mood of the occasion.
3. Beware of sentiment and reminiscence taking the place of a constructive message.
4. Be realistic in your appraisal of heroes.
5. Check on the possibility of employing a doctrinal emphasis.
6. Avoid trite phrases and cliches.
7. Beware of getting so intrigued in the minutiae of the message that you miss its practicality.
8. Deliver the message with enthusiasm.
9. Use curios and maps in presenting a missionary message.
10. Have something in your message for all ages and groups represented in the audience.
11. Do not place yourself unnecessarily on the side of an issue which will divide your listeners.
12. Do not spend a lot of time discussing the obvious.
13. The presentation will be aided by having a story as the core of your message.
14. Remember that you are a specialist only in your own area.

1. Consider the Chronological Relationship

ADVENT SUNDAY (Sunday Nearest Nov. 30)
    Advent Sunday
    Universal Bible Sunday   (Four Sundays)
    Prophet's Sunday   ADVENT SEASON
    Forerunner's Sunday

CHRISTMAS DAY (December 25)   (Eight Days) CHRISTMASTIDE
EPIPHANY DAY (January 6)
    (Six Sundays — Maximum)   EPIPHANY SEASON

ASH WEDNESDAY   Forty Days Plus Six Sundays Before Easter)
  40 Days   (Six Sundays Plus Forty Days)   LENTEN SEASON
    Passiontide (Last Two Weeks of Lent)
      Passion Sunday (Fifth Sunday of Lent)
      Palm Sunday (Sixth Sunday of Lent)
        Holy Week (Week Before Easter)
        Maundy Thursday
        Good Friday

EASTER SUNDAY   (May be as early as March 22 or as late as April 25)
  40 Days   EASTERTIDE
    Rogation Sunday — Rural Life Sunday
    (Fifth Sunday after Easter)

ASCENSION DAY
  50 Days   "The Great Fifty Days"   ASCENSIONTIDE
PENTECOST (Seventh Sunday after Easter)
  7 Days   WHITSUNTIDE
TRINITY SUNDAY   (Eighth Sunday after Easter)
    (Last Sunday of August until Advent)   KINGDOMTIDE

PRESENTATION 101

2. Consider the Special Emphases of the Months of the Year

January ....*Special Emphasis:* Bible Study
   Jan. 1 – Day of Prayer   Missionary Sunday
   Jan. 6 – Epiphany Day   Christian Education Week
   Jan. 25 – Forefather's Day National Youth Week
      First Week: Week of Prayer

February ....*Special Emphasis:* Christian Education
   Feb. 14 – Sweethearts' Day
      First Sunday: Boy Scout and Youth
      Second Sunday: Brotherhood and Race Relations
                     Christian World Fellowship
      Third Sunday: Christian Education

March ....*Special Emphasis:* Home Missions
      First Sunday: National Missions

April .... *Special Emphases:* Life Commitment
                                     Christian Vocation
   April 19 – Patriots' Day
      First Sunday: Renewal
        Life Commitment
        Christian Stewardship

May ....*Special Emphasis:* Christian Home
   May 30 – Memorial Day
      First Week: Christian Family
      Second Sunday: Mother's Day
      National Music Week

June ....*Special Emphases:* Youth
                            Vacation Bible School
      First Sunday: Christian Unity
      Second Sunday: Children's Day
      Third Sunday: Father's Day
      Last Sunday: Nature
        Flag Day
        Trinity Sunday

July ....*Special Emphases:* Church Encampments
                              Christian Recreation
                              Christian Literature
   July 4 – Independence Day
      Second Sunday: Christian Literature
        Freedom Sunday

August .... *Special Emphases:* Leadership Enlistment
Church Library
Church Renewal
August 6 — Transfiguration Day
August 15 — Assumption Day
Friendship Day

September .... *Special Emphasis:* Church Program Planning
First Monday: Labor Day
Second Sunday: Public Education and College Sunday
Third Sunday: Church Rally Day
Last Sunday: Leadership Commitment Sunday
Last Week: Church Preparation and Program Planning
National Home Week
National Fall Sunday School Week

October .... *Special Emphasis:* Teaching and Training
in Church Membership
October 12 — Columbus Day
October 31 — Reformation Day
First Full Week: Christian Education Week
First Sunday: Worldwide Communion Sunday
Third Sunday: Laymen's Sunday
National Bible Week
Girl Scout Week

November .... *Special Emphases:* Christian Stewardship
Men and Missions
International Good Will
Nov. 1 — All Saints Day
Nov. 11 — Armistice Day (Veterans Day)
Second Sunday: World Peace Sunday
Fourth Thursday: Thanksgiving Day
American Education Week   Stewardship Sunday
National Book Week   Election Day

December .... *Special Emphases:* World (Foreign) Missions
Worldwide Bible Reading
Dec. 15 — Bill of Rights Day
Dec. 25 — Christmas Day

3. Consider the Special Days

(Scripture references here are some of those suggested
by some denominations for reading on that day.)

Advent Sunday

This is the first Sunday of the Christian year and the first Sunday
in the Advent Season. It is the Sunday nearest November 30. This

is the beginning of the special season of preparation for the coming birth of Christ.
>Rom. 13:8-14
>Matt. 2:1-9

All Saints Day
> This comes on November 1 and was established first by Boniface IV in the seventh century. It is the day for memorializing the departed faithful.

Armistice Day
> This is also known as Veterans Day and occurs on November 11.

Ascension Day (See *Manual*, p. 191.)
> This is the first Sunday in Ascensiontide and comes forty days after Easter. It marks the beginning of the season of preparation for Pentecost. The close of Ascensiontide ends the first half of the Christian year.
>> Acts 1:1-11
>> Mark 16:14-20
>> Luke 24:49-53

Ash Wednesday (See *Manual*, p. 194.)
> This comes forty days and six Sundays before Easter. It was established as a day of special observance by Pope Gregory I in the sixth century. It marks the beginning of the season of preparation for the proper celebration of Easter.
>> Joel 2:12-19
>> Matt. 6:16-21

Bill of Rights Day
> This is observed on December 15.

Black Friday
> This is the Friday before Easter and marks the day of observance of the crucifixion of Christ.
>> Exod. 12:1-11
>> Heb. 10:1-25

Boy Scout Sunday
> This and Youth Sunday are observed on the first Sunday of February.

Brotherhood Sunday
> This and Race Relations Sunday are observed on the second Sunday of February.

Cantate Sunday
> This is the name given to the fourth Sunday after Easter. The

introit for the day is the first verse of the cantate, the 98th Psalm. It may be observed as a festival of sacred music and hymns.

Children's Day (See *Manual*, p. 172.)
This is normally observed on the second Sunday of June. Children's sermons were discussed by the two following homiletics writers:
Caldwell, *Preaching Angles*, pp. 80, 81.
Kidder, *A Treatise on Homiletics*, pp. 284-291.

Christian Unity Day
This is observed on the first Sunday of June.

Christmas Sunday (See *Manual*, p. 196.)
This is the Sunday prior to Christmas Day which is December 25.

Day of Prayer
January 1 is often observed as a day of prayer and the first week of January is regarded as a week of prayer.

Easter Sunday (See *Manual*, p. 192.)
This may be observed as early as March 22 or as late as April 25.
Mark 16:1-8
John 20:1-10

Epiphany Day, also called *Twelfth Day*
This comes on January 6 and is the first day of Epiphany Season which extends for a maximum of six Sundays. It is a festival commemorating the manifestation of Christ to the Gentiles represented by the Magi.

Expectation Sunday
This is another name for Ascension Sunday which is the Sunday after Ascension Day.
John 15:26 – 16:4a
I Peter 4:7-11

Family Day (See *Manual*, p. 174.)
Christian Family Week is observed during the first full week of May.

Father and Son Week
This is observed during the first full week of November.

Father's Day (See *Manual*, p. 175.)
This is the third Sunday of June.

Forefather's Day
This is observed on December 21 or January 25 in recognition of

PRESENTATION 105

    the landing of the Pilgrims in 1620.
    I Peter 2:4-8 — The Pilgrim's Rock

Good Friday (See *Manual*, p. 193.)
    This is the Friday before Easter and marks the observance of the crucifixion of Christ.
    John 18:1 — 19:42

Independence Day (See *Manual*, p. 163.)
    This is celebrated on July 4.

International Good Will Day
    This day is observed in November.

Labor Day (See *Manual*, p. 164.)
    This is the first Monday in September.

Lenten Sundays
    These are the six Sundays coming between Ash Wednesday and Easter.

Lincoln's Birthday (See *Manual*, p. 165.)
    This is observed on February 12.

Maundy Thursday
    This is the Thursday prior to Easter and is often the time for the observance of pre-Easter communion. It is the commemoration of the washing of the disciples' feet.
    Luke 23:1-49
    I Cor. 11:23-32

Memorial Day (See *Manual*, p. 153.)
    This comes on May 30.

Men and Missions Sunday
    In 1930 the Laymen's Missionary Movement set aside the third Sunday of November.

Missionary Day
    This is observed on the second Sunday after Epiphany.
    Mark 1:1-11
    Rom. 12:6-16

Mother's Day
    This is the second Sunday of May.

Nature Day
    This is sometimes observed on the first Sunday and sometimes on the last Sunday of June.

Palm Sunday

This is the Sunday before Easter and marks the observance of the Triumphal Entry of Christ into Jerusalem.
Matt. 21:1-9

Passion Sunday
This is the fifth Sunday in Lent and is also known as Black Sunday.
John 8:46-59
Heb. 9:11-15

Pentecost or *Whitsunday* (See *Manual*, p. 195.)
This is the seventh Sunday after Easter and is the first of seven days known as Whitsuntide. It is one of the oldest of the Christian celebrations going back to the three principal feasts of Judaism.

Race Relations Day
This and Brotherhood Sunday are observed on the second Sunday of February.

Red Cross Day
This day is observed in November.

Reformation Day
This is observed on October 31 and commemorates Luther's signing of the Theses.

Religious Education Week
In 1930 the first full week of October was designated for the purpose of stressing religious education.

Renewal Sunday or *Lord's Day-Alliance Day*
This is the second Sunday after Easter.
John 10:11-16
I Peter 2:19-25

Rogation Day or *Rural Life Sunday*
This is the fifth Sunday after Easter. This and the following days were special times for praying for crops. The name comes from a Latin verb meaning "to beseech."

Septuagesima Sunday
This comes seventy days before Easter and represents a time of preparation for the observance of Easter.
Matt. 20:1-16
I Cor. 9:24 — 10:5

Shrove Monday
This is the Monday before Ash Wednesday. It was the early feast day before the final fast of Lent. It is a day of confession.

PRESENTATION 107

Stewardship Day
This is normally observed in the month of November.

Thanksgiving Day (See *Manual*, p. 166.)
This is observed on the fourth Thursday of November.

Trinity Sunday
This is a festival in honor of the Trinity and is observed on the eighth Sunday after Easter and the First Sunday after Pentecost.
Rom. 11:33-36
I John 4:8-21.

Universal Bible Sunday (See *Manual*, p. 180.)
This is observed on the second Sunday of Advent Season.
Romans 15:4-12

Veteran's Day (See *Manual*, p. 167.)
This is also known as Armistice Day and is observed on November 11.

Vocation Day
This comes on the second Sunday after Easter and stresses the Christian teaching regarding life work.

Watchnight Service (See *Manual*, p. 181.)
This service is held on New Year's Eve.

World Peace Day
This is observed on the second Sunday of November.

World Day of Prayer
This is observed on the first Friday of Lent.

Worldwide Communion Sunday
In 1939, the first Sunday of October was established as the Worldwide Communion Sunday.

Youth Day
This and Boy Scout Sunday are observed on the first Sunday of February.

4. Consider the Special Occasions

Anniversary Occasion (See *Manual*, p. 168.)
Preaching on such an occasion is discussed in the following book:
Riley, *The Preacher and His Preaching*, p. 79.
Sermon Ideas:
Ps. 27:1-14 — Wait and See
John 21:15-23 — Learning By Experience

Baccalaureate (See *Manual,* p. 156.)
  Sermon Ideas:
    Acts 26:13-28 — Almost
    II Cor. 12:10 — Transformed Limitation

Banquet Occasion (See *Manual,* p. 169.)
  Sermon Ideas:
    Prov. 13:1-11 — The Source of Wealth
    Heb. 3:7-13 — The Peril of Procrastination

Baptism (See *Manual,* p. 170.)
  Sermon Ideas:
    Col. 3:1-4 — The Center of the Christian Life
    Heb. 11:23-28 — Life's Choices

Bible Conference (See *Manual,* p. 171.)
  Sermon Ideas:
    Hos. — The Gospel from a Broken Heart
    II Peter 1:5-9 — Progressive Piety

Children's Home (See *Manual,* p. 157.)
  Preaching to children is discussed in the following books:
    Blackwood, *The Preparation of Sermons,* pp. 234-241.
    Kern, *The Ministry to the Congregation,* pp. 425-440.
    Kidder, *A Treatise on Homiletics,* pp. 284-291.
    Patton, *The Preparation and Delivery of Sermons,* pp. 159-161.
    Riley, *The Preacher and His Preaching,* pp. 84, 85.
  Sermon Ideas:
    Mark 9:33-37 — Learning from a Child
    Luke 18:15-17 — A Child's Friend

Church Dedication (See *Manual,* p. 173.)
  Sermon Ideas:
    II Chron. 5:14 — The House of God was Full
    II Chron. 6:12 — A Prayer for this House

College Chapel Service (See *Manual,* p. 158.)
  Sermon Ideas:
    I Kings 3:3-15 — A Wise Man's Prayer
    John 18:15-38 — Warming at the Devil's Fire

Commencement Service
  If this is to be observed on a Sunday, it will normally take place on the second Sunday in June.
  Sermon Ideas:
    Ps. 111:10 — The Beginning of Wisdom
    Heb. 10:32-39 — Press On

PRESENTATION 109

Communion Service (See *Manual*, p. 176.)
   Sermon Ideas:
      I Cor. 11:23-29 — This Do In Remembrance
      I John 3:13-24 — The Art of Loving

Denominational Convention (See *Manual*, p. 183.)
   Sermon Ideas:
      Acts 2:37-47 — A Pattern for Progress
      Heb. 12:1-13 — The Race of a Lifetime

Family Reunion (See *Manual*, p. 151.)
   Sermon Ideas:
      Matt. 5:1-12 — A Formula for Happiness
      I Cor. 16:19-20 — The Church in Thy House

Fund Raising Rally (See *Manual*, p. 152.)
   Sermon Ideas:
      Phil. 1:21 — What Life Really Means
      James 1:14-21 — God, the Great Giver

Funeral (See *Manual*, p. 189, 190.)
   Sermon Ideas:
      Deut. 31:7, 8 — Secure in God
      John 14:1-18 — The Secret of an Untroubled Heart

High School Assembly (See *Manual*, p. 159.)
   Sermon Ideas:
      Judg. 12:1-6 — Thy Speech Betrayeth Thee
      I Sam. 17:12-58 — Fighting Giants

Home for the Aged (See *Manual*, p. 160.)
   Sermon Ideas:
      Ps. 46 — Blessed Assurance
      Heb. 13:1-6 — A Triumphant Assurance

Military Post (See *Manual*, p. 186.)
   Sermon Ideas:
      Acts 8:26-40 — Called to Active Duty
      Heb. 10:26-31 — Keep Your Confidence

Minister's Conference (See *Manual*, p. 184.)
   Sermon Ideas:
      Eph. 3:14-19 — A Preacher's Prayer
      Matt. 26:30-75 — Portrait of an Inconsistent Life

Missionary Conference (See *Manual*, p. 177.)
   Preaching missionary messages is discussed in the following books:

Johnson, *The Ideal Ministry,* pp. 368-371.
Kern, *The Ministry to the Congregation,* p. 411.
Kidder, *A Treatise on Homiletics,* pp. 281-283, 375-377.
Patton, *The Preparation and Delivery of Sermons,* p. 153.
Sermon Ideas:
    Matt. 9:35-38 — The Compulsion of Compassion
    Acts 13:1-51 — The Holy Spirit and Missions

Open Air Meeting (See *Manual,* p. 187.)
Preaching on such an occasion is discussed in the following books:
    Byington, *Open Air Preaching,* (Entire book).
    Etter, *The Preacher and His Sermon,* pp. 231-235.
Sermon Ideas:
    Luke 19:1-10 — Get off the Limb
    Matt. 19:16-30 — Not for Sale

Ordination Service (See *Manual,* p. 179.)
Sermon Ideas:
    Gen. 37:5-11 — Joseph, A Dreamer of Dreams
    I Tim. 3:1-7 — Needed, Qualified Ministers

Parent Teachers Association Meeting (See *Manual,* p. 154.)
Sermon Ideas:
    Deut. 6:1-23 — Molding Our Future
    I Sam. 1:1-20 — As a Twig is Bent
    I Peter 2:11 — 3:7 — A Christian's Responsibility Toward Society

Prayer Meeting
Sermon Ideas:
    I Kings 8:22-54 — The Parts of Prayer
    Phil. 1:1-12 — Joy in Prayer

Prison (See *Manual,* p. 161.)
Sermon Ideas:
    Ps. 139:1-6 — Who Told God?
    John 8:21-36 — Made Free

Professional or Commercial Convention (See *Mannual,* p. 150.)
Sermon Ideas:
    Ps. 37:1-15 — Tired of Tension?
    I Peter 1:13-22 — The Central Interest of Life

Service Club (See *Manual,* p. 155.)
Sermon Ideas:
    I Chron. 28:1-10 — Called to Serve
    Ps. 90:12 — Numbering Our Days

Shop or Factory Service (See *Manual*, p. 188.)
    Sermon Ideas:
        Matt. 20:1-16 — A Labor Dispute
        John 15 — A Parable of Production

Sunday School Worker's Conference (See *Manual*, p. 185.)
    Sermon Ideas:
        II Kings 22:1-20 — Making Our Influence Count
        I Peter 2 — Christian Conduct in a Confused World

Theological Seminary Chapel (See *Manual*, p. 162.)
    Sermon Ideas:
        I Sam. 12 — The Eloquence of Life
        Acts 3 — What's in a Name?

Wedding (See *Manual*, p. 182.)
    Sermon Ideas:
        Mark 10:2-9 — What God Hath Joined
        Eph. 3:14-21 — Love in Four Dimensions

B. Employ Different Methods of Presentation

The majority of parish preachers deliver their *messages from notes*. Notes of the proper kind interpose little mental barrier between the speaker and the hearer. Notes prepared should be brief and written in such a way that they can be read at a glance. The words should be well separated. Indentation, the use of capitals, and helpful underlining will make them easier to grasp. In order to preach from notes effectively, one must learn to use them advantageously. A well-organized outline will make it easier for memorization and will take away the necessity for having so many notes that they become embarrassing. There should not be so many notes that it is necessary for the speaker to turn a page while delivering the message. The exception to this rule would come when there was a unique occasion demanding exacting language but not a manuscript. Do not have the notes in an unattached form on the pulpit. The preacher should not yield to the temptation to include long quotations, poems, hymns, etc. within the notes which will demand direct reading. He should only include that which can be memorized or grasped in a glance.

Some preachers have a special gift for *memorizing* and find that they can memorize their message for presentation. This was the favorite method employed by the ancient rhetoricians. They cultivated their memories. One of the five divisions of classical rhetoric beyond invention, arrangement, style, and delivery was that of memory. This type of delivery has never been as popular in America as it has been in England and Scotland. It is advocated, however, for the occasional or exceptional sermon where freedom of delivery may be combined with carefulness, thoroughness, accuracy of thought, and diction. There is a modified type of memorized message to which we should call attention. In this, a few sections of the message such as the introduction are memorized but the great bulk of the message is given with some notes or extemporaneously without direct verbal recall.

If a preacher is going to deliver his message from a *manuscript*, he should obtain some training in the oral interpretation of literature as well as in public speaking. There are occasions for reading from a manuscript when no other method is as good. These are the times when it is important to speak carefully, to choose one's words carefully, and to stay within very limited time boundaries. A radio message, for instance, should be delivered from manuscript. The practice of reading sermons as a frequent thing is generally believed to have originated in the reign of Henry VIII. It is imperative that the preacher read and reread the manuscript until he is saturated with it and can then lose himself in the ardor of preaching. It is necessary to concentrate on maintaining eye contact as much as possible. In preparing the manuscript, it is wise to transcribe that which you would normally say, thus giving it oral style rather than the style of an essay. The presentation of the sermon should be marked by vivid gesticulation, concrete illustrations, and vocal variety.

The presentation of a message *without notes* demands thorough preparation. The extempore method of preaching was universal in the first centuries of Christianity and was the chosen method of the reformers. There are several dangers connected with this type of presentation. There is the temptation toward inadequate preparation, both mental and spiritual. The tendency to repeat is also present. Some tend to substitute words for solid thoughts. There is also the danger that the speaker will become too dependent upon his momentary feelings. There is always the possibility of mistaking fluency for extemporaneous ability. A concise logical outline is one of the primary requirements for one who desires to present a sermon without notes in the pulpit. The sermon should be practiced orally before it is delivered to the congregation.

There are special types of sermons which demand special forms of delivery. Jones, in his book, *Principles and Practice of Preaching*, pp. 113, 114, refers to the *imaginary conversation sermon* and the *autobiographical monologue sermon*. Kidder in his book, *A Treatise on Homiletics*, pp. 272, 273, refers to the *hortatory sermon*.

The *dramatic sermon* places a scene before the congregation with all of the characters talking and acting naturally. It is a dramatized sermon. Mark refers to this type in his book, *Patterns for Preaching*, pp. 44-48.

The *illustrated sermon* was discussed by four authors:
   Breed, *Preparing to Preach,* pp. 437-446.
   Etter, *The Preacher and His Sermon,* pp. 224-227.
   Fisk, *Manual Preaching,* pp. 213-223.
   Phelps, *Theory of Preaching,* p. 34.
This sermon involves the use of a map, chart, or other material in connection with the presentation of the sermon. It may also involve the making of a deeper impression of Biblical truth through the delineation of a Bible character. This type of message is especially effective with a believing audience.

C. Adjust the Type of Presentation to the Type of Audience

The speaker should recognize the type of audience before which he is presenting his message and should make any needed adjustments. There are five types of audiences in terms of the occasion. The *pedestrian audience* challenges the speaker to catch their attention and to maintain their interest. The *passive audience* presents as its main challenge the maintaining of interest. The *selected audience*, which has assembled because of a common purpose, challenges the speaker to make an impression of the subject on their mind and memory, to motivate them, and to direct their action. The *concerted audience* is one which has an active purpose. That audience must be motivated and have its action directed. The fifth type of audience is the *organized one.* In this case, the speaker's task is to direct their action.

There are four types of audiences in terms of their interests and their attitudes toward the speaker and his ideas. These four are the *apathetic,* the *believing,* the *doubtful,* and the *hostile* audience.

There are three reasons for believing anything. The first is that of the sensory in which we believe because we can see it. The second is that of authority where the individual believes because it was told to him. The final reason for believing is that of reasoning or argumentation in that it has been proven.

When dealing with a *believing audience,* one should emphasize the sensory material, use some authority material, and very little, if any, reasoning material. The *doubting audience* wants reasoning material, some authority information, but very little sensory material. The *hostile audience* demands much authority information, some reasoning material, and no sensory content. The *apathetic audience* presents a unique challenge in that one must get and hold its attention and then as soon as this is done it becomes one of the three preceding types and the appropriate approach must then be used.

1. The Apathetic Audience

The physical factors in the speaking situation take on special significance when the apathetic audience is involved. Some of the factors are outside of the control of the speaker. There are others, however, which he may alter providing he is aware of methods of improvement.

It will be helpful to polarize the audience. This can be done by having them seated close together. They should be encouraged to enter into joint participation in laughing, singing, and sharing in a common ritual. If the speaker emphasizes near the beginning of his speech the matters on which the audience has common agreement, this will tend to draw the audience together. The stress should be upon the unanimity of feeling which exists among the auditors.

All distractions should be removed from the speaking area. A choir seated behind the speaker or participants on the platform during the message can distract the audience.

There should be a concentration of light centered upon the speaker. This should be located so that it does not reflect upon glasses and should be of such coloring that it does not give a sallow complexion to the speaker. Avoid dimming the lights in the congregation during the message. It is imperative that the speaker see his audience if he desires to persuade them, capture their attention, and maintain their interest.

A high speaking platform will work to the disadvantage of the speaker. It gives the auditors the impression that the speaker is separated from them and does not desire to be on their level. Such a platform will encourage the audience to doze while the speaker is delivering his message. This is due to the fact that the eyes will be encouraged to roll upward and backward as when one sleeps.

The correct temperature level and proper ventilation are two important factors. The temperature level should be set at about 68 degrees before the audience arrives. It will then lift to a height of 72 degrees during the message. Plenty of fresh air should be available.

Any motor activity on the part of the speaker helps to get the attention of the audience. There are some guides, however, which should be followed. The speaker should not rush to the lectern and begin speaking at once. It is better to approach the speaking location in a deliberate and poised manner. He should then stand for just a moment before beginning to speak. This will in itself help to get the attention of the auditors and will at the same time help to break the tension in the body of the speaker. It is normally wise to avoid gestures in the introduction. They will accomplish more in the remaining portions of the speech. There is no such thing as an awkward gesture providing you gesture while speaking. The absence of gestures will produce dips in attention. Freedom is the rule in front

PRESENTATION 115

of an audience. Avoid activity which merely indicates the nervous condition of the speaker but does not enhance the presentation of the material.

The first few minutes of a speech are of special importance. It is well, therefore, to know how to choose the ideas and content of the message. In the introduction it is wise to avoid abstract generalizations, a long rambling history of the subject, or the exposition of the background knowledge necessary for an understanding of your speech. Avoid over-elaborate preliminaries and definitions. It is not wise to begin a message with an apology. As a rule, one should avoid giving all the message away in the introduction.

An effective introduction will be short, presented with quiet confidence, and be characterized by variation in delivery. The following ideas and types of material are helpful in gaining and holding attention. Humorous material is disarming and provides a relief from the strained tension of attention. That which is novel or unusual gets attention. People have a tendency to listen to material which pertains to familiar homely doings. If you tell the old with a novel twist, you will make a positive claim for their attention. Action and conflict material maintains interest. Material which is timely will attract their interest. This is especially true if it touches the audience directly. The auditors will pay special attention when the speaker provides inside information which is not shared with the public at large. Listeners are interested in becoming involved in larger enterprises. They have a tendency to listen to human interest material. This involves eccentricities of all kinds. Heart interest material such as stories of struggles, defeats, and victories have a special appeal.

It has been said that there are two chief causes of ineffectiveness. These are indirectness and "monomood." When dealing with an apathetic audience and attempting to gain and hold their attention, the speaker should avoid these two items.

2. *The Believing Audience*

The believing audience is often a passive audience. It accepts the position held by the speaker but fails to respond to his pleas for acceptance and action. If the speaker uses a *didactic approach* with such an audience, he will fail to arouse them. Such an approach declares flatly that which he wants and wants done. It has a tendency toward vagueness, generality, and abstraction. There are principles and generalizations without the specifics. The speech is saturated with conclusions without adequate indication as to why or how the speaker arrived at such positions. This type of approach assumes that the listener can make the leap from the principle to the application. It lacks the arts of attractiveness.

The *dramatic approach* is the one which is advocated when speaking to a believing audience. Such an audience is exemplified in the typical prayer meeting attendants or the audience at a missionary conference. The challenge is to deepen the impression.

There are eight suggestions which, when put together, form the dramatic approach in the presentation of material. The first suggestion is that the speech contain a maximum of illustrations and a minimum of principles. This will assist the audience in seeing specifically that which you are trying to convey. It is wise to employ visual aids. Theoretically every idea can be visualized. These should not be used for their own sake but rather with the purpose of conveying the thrust of the message. In order to be effective, they must be visible to all. If they are too interesting, the speaker may find that they will detract from the impact of the message rather than enhance it. The third suggestion is to obtain audience participation. One simple way of doing this is to have them respond to questions. One must be certain, however, to avoid embarrassment to the ones responding. Facts and details will be more impressive if presented in clusters. A series of statistics will tend to draw the attention of the listener to that point in the message. The fifth suggestion encourages the employment of examples and anecdotes. Such illustrations will reduce fatigue. They will assist in visualizing the point. Without examples, no principles really make sense. In the average speech we should move in cycles from the abstract to the concrete and back again. In dramatizing the idea before a believing audience, it is wise to stay in the concrete. The skillful use of indirection will aid the speaker. Instead of directly telling the audience, the speaker employs the approach advocated by Bishop Whately and presents the idea obliquely. He introduces circumstances connected with the main object and event and affected by it, but not absolutely forming a part of it. The seventh suggestion emphasizes the importance of making use of comparisons, similes, and metaphors. A comparison involves an attempt to compare objects which have many qualities in common. A simile is the most used figure of speech. It is an attempt to compare things essentially unlike except in certain aspects. The metaphor is the figure of speech which Aristotle felt was the most important. It is an imaginative identification of one object with another or the ascribing to something the qualities of something else. A metaphor is a concealed simile. The final suggestion emphasizes the importance of using the telling detail. This is the little detail which the average person would tend to overlook. We should be specific in our description of each item referred to within the speech.

3. *The Doubtful Audience*

The doubtful audience is one which has not as yet formed definite opinions. They need to see the weight of the data. There is a necessity to show the validity of the argument itself without injecting too much of the personality of the speaker. The speaker must be able to talk factually, make predictions, develop theories, and draw conclusions.

General Semantics, which involves a study of language, facts, and human evaluations, has made valuable contributions in this area of talking factually. The philosophical foundation for General Semantics is logical positivism. The Biblical sermonizer should evaluate the declarations and teachings of the General Semanticist with this fact in mind. We take for granted that what we say will be factual. The General Semanticist reminds us that inferences can be made anytime, often go beyond that which is actually seen, merely manifest a degree of probability, and can be actually unlimited in number. In contrast, facts can only be made after observation. They must not go beyond that which has been observed. They approach certainty. Because of their exacting nature, they tend to be limited in number. We should not expect that the speaker will use only facts and avoid inferences. We should expect, however, that he will not try to give inferences to the audience and imply that such are facts. The grammatical structure of a given sentence gives no clue actually as to the factuality of the statement.

The speaker should avoid giving the impression to the audience that what he has said upon a given subject is all which can be said upon it. There is nothing in the world in which complexity may not be obtained. We abstract from this totality on the basis of our limitations of time, usefulness, and learning. We can raise difficult problems when we fail to recognize or fail to let our audience know that we are abstracting or selecting from a wide range of possible material. There is still more information.

It is important to remember that when we are dealing with people all situations present complexities. This can be sensed when we realize that no two people are alike and consequently their reactions cannot be predicted.

Time changes situations and individuals. We often fail to date our statements. We should avoid distortions of the facts by making certain that we give the time orientation for the statements and that these are conveyed to the listener.

There is a tendency in English to overemphasize similarities and overlook differences. We thus distort the picture of the world in which we live and make it difficult to see variety as it exists. In dealing with a doubtful audience we should strive to fix the variables by giving the specifics of identification. This achievement of precision involves speaking with a high degree of rigor.

It is easy to drift into a pattern of speaking in terms of the extremes of life. This is not, however, true to the facts of life. Speaking in terms of extremes is oversimplification. We should discover the gradations and thereby lessen the possibility of conflict.

Not all conversation is designed for maximum rigor. Phatic communion is any talking between individuals which is designed to bridge the private bounds of loneliness. Such conversation does not aim at instruction but rather at preventing silence. It is the individual's attempt to break through the barrier of isolation and make contact with others. Unless this type of speaking is recognized for what it really is, great misunderstanding may result.

It is not only important to talk factually with a doubtful audience, it is also important to be able to make predictions. It is important that the speaker satisfy the tests of authority if he wants the listener to rely on his prediction. It is not enough to say that someone stated it, therefore, it must be true. Humanly speaking, there is no such thing as a certain prediction, therefore, we should not give the impression of certainty to the listener. The speaker must assure the audience that he has control over the variables connected with the prediction. This degree of control must be made clear. There should be no hesitancy on the part of the speaker in telling the audience how he arrived at his present point of view. The speaker may use special pleading. This involves the giving of a number of examples which just serve this point. In the use of special pleading, the contradictions will appear to be very few in the light of the examples presented.

The speaker should develop the ability to formulate theories. A theory combines a number of inferences and is an attempt to provide a statement that will cover aspects of phenomena which seem to be observable. All proposals require a theory in order to get a solution. Since any theory is a matter of probability, we must assure the audience of the extent of coverage of our theory. It must be shown that no alternative theory can account for the resulting phenomena.

The search for causes always involves probabilities and inferences. We can never see a cause but only the consequences. When speaking before a doubtful audience, the speaker must be able to deny the coincidences, in other words, show that it was not a mere coincidence. He should establish that it was a controlling factor. This means that the change could not have taken place without it. He must establish with high probability that no other controlling factors were involved.

4. *The Hostile Audience*

When a speaker is dealing with a hostile audience, it is helpful to develop a response to yourself as a person. This involves establishing your authority to speak. This may be done first of all by invoking the authority of others. The speaker adopts a neutral delivery and becomes a mouthpiece for another. He just wants to tell the audience what great men have thought upon the question before them. He may proceed to prove that the authority which he is quoting is qualified to speak. He can do this by showing that he has the signs of respectability. Four of these signs include being a professor in the field, having adequate educational background, belonging to learned organizations, and finally having written a textbook in the field. It is helpful to show that the authority is in agreement with authorities of equal stature. You can establish his special competency to be an authority by showing that he is in a position to know the facts. The speaker may establish the credibility of his authority by showing how many times he has been right in the past.

There are several ways in which the speaker can establish his own prestige or authority before a hostile audience. His force, vitality, poise, and confidence will go far in that direction. His sincerity, sympathy, kindness, and compassion will enhance his presentation. The enormity of his cultural background and depth of personality will be positive factors. Thoroughness of preparation is important. It must be evident that the speaker has thought through his material to the point where it has become a part of him.

The speaker should show respect for his audience. He should not be pompous and patronizing nor should he be too deferential and obsequious. It is wise to recognize the identity of the particular audience by making specific reference to it. The speaker may reveal his personal enjoyment in being present for the speaking occasion. It is important to manifest fairness toward one's opponents. The speaker should concede as much as possible. He should avoid habitual overstatements and avoid cultivating a pattern of understatements. If the speaker compliments the audience, it is best to use indirect compliments.

A speaker may select one of five approaches to use with a hostile audience. The first of these might be called the "common ground" approach. In this he makes use of all of the areas in which he as the speaker and the audience have a point of common interest and endeavor. The second has been termed the blind or circuitous approach. The speaker discusses matters which are only indirectly related to his basic idea to which the audience is hostile. When some of this hostility has been worn away by waiting, then the disturbing idea is presented. The speaker may begin his message with a series of questions to which the audience will give quiet assent within their minds. The inductive approach is one which presents a series of cases without drawing any conclusion. The conclusion should hopefully be apparent and thus be drawn by the audience. This conclusion will have a carry-over and bearing upon the idea to which the listeners have been hostile. The fifth approach is that of absolute candor. It is here that the speaker states his purpose openly and then appeals to the intelligence and sportsmanship of the listeners.

D. Incorporate Dialogue in the Presentation

Some serious charges are being made against traditional preaching. It has been said that the language is complex and archaic. Many feel that much of the material is irrelevant and uninteresting. There is great question in many quarters as to whether or not preaching is producing results which are in proportion to the emphasis placed upon it and the time spent in its preparation and presentation.

Communication is a dynamic process in which individuals must share experiences and ideas. Effective communication depends upon feedback. We are not achieving the purposes of communication by merely giving our answers to people's questions or by merely securing concensus with the point of view of the communicator. If we are to communicate, we must be willing to listen. We can only then convey information and meaning as well as help people make responsible decisions.

The church faces a changing world. The clergyman is no longer the cornerstone of the community. The intellectual level of the congregation has changed. The parishioner now knows that what he thinks and believes is important. The members of the congregation are increasingly impatient with those structures in which he is only a passive spectator.

The incorporation of dialogue in the presentation would bring a change of method without having to make a change in the subject matter of the message. The following methods are being tried with varying degrees of effectiveness.

1. A discussion period is held following the sermon. The minister stays for a few minutes to clarify items and then leaves, thus encouraging freedom of discussion by the parishioners.
2. The midweek service consists of a short worship period and message. The congregation then leaves the sanctuary and goes downstairs for coffee and a discussion period. The benediction is not pronounced until the close of the discussion period.
3. Some churches provide two or three options for the attendants following the worship service. They may attend a large discussion group on some social or personal problem related to the sermon. They may select a Bible study session. The third option is to attend the youth discussion period.
4. A group of parishioners can meet with the pastor during the week to discuss the message to be delivered on the following Lord's Day.
5. Small Bible study groups can meet to study the Bible passage

PRESENTATION

which will form the foundation for the next message by the pastor.

6. Groups may meet to discuss the ways in which the Gospel relates to a particular task or problem.

There needs to be an emphasis upon the responsibility of every Christian to share his faith and to witness to it in the midst of his fellow Christians. The dialogue structure can be one in which feelings and concerns can be shared and trust emerge.

METHODS OF INCORPORATING DIALOGUE*

BEFORE THE SERMON

1. *Private Study*
   —based on advance assignments of preaching portions
2. *Small Groups*
   —preaching portion of next Sunday's sermon is discussed
3. *Sermon Seminar*
   —pastor gives a sermonic explanation of next Sunday's preaching portion re:
     context
     comments
       (exegetical)
     concern
       (proposition)
   —groups reduce content to principles, see implications, make varied applications
   —pastor circulates to get sermonic help
4. *Sermon Board*
   —composed of 8 representative members
   —members rotate quarterly
   —pastor meets weekly to discuss previously assigned preaching portions in light of the question: "What do I need to say to you from this portion?"

DURING THE SERMON

1. *One-Man, One-Voice Dialogue*
   —due to correlative preparation pastor is able to anticipate the people's questions which they would ask if they could
   —causes internal interaction
2. *Dialogue Sermon*
   —2 or more give the message: 1 from the pulpit and 1 from the audience; 2 from separate pulpits; one speaking for God, one for Satan, and one for man
3. *Discussion Sermon*
   —members of the congregation interact verbally with the pastor and with each other
4. *Lay Preaching*
   —Principle: the congregation preaches to itself

AFTER THE SERMON

1. *After Service Forum*
   —in place of SS
   —after evening service
   —discussion on the content and application of the sermon
2. *Talk-Back Sermon*
   —pastor preaches in the morning
   —people reply in the evening
3. *Feedback Group*
   —sermon seminar reconvenes to evaluate without the pastor
   —questions:
     (1) What did this sermon say to you?
     (2) What difference, if any, do you think the message will make in your life?
     (3) In what ways did the pastor help or hinder in the presentation of his thought?
   —session is taped for the pastor to hear later

*Prepared by Wesley Pinkham

BIBLIOGRAPHY

BIBLIOGRAPHY

1. Baxter, Batsell B. *Speaking for the Master.* New York: Macmillan Co., 1954, 134 pp.
2. Blackwood, Andrew W. *Doctrinal Preaching for Today.* New York: Abingdon Press, 1956, 224 pp.
3. _____. *Planning a Year's Pulpit Work.* New York: Abingdon Press, 1943, 240 pp.
4. _____. *Preaching from the Bible.* New York: Abingdon-Cokesbury Press, 1946.
5. _____. *The Preparation of Sermons.* New York: Abingdon-Cokesbury Press, 1948, 272 pp. (inc. index).
6. Brastow, Lewis O. *The Work of the Preacher: A Study of Homiletic Principles and Methods.* New York: Pilgrim Press, 1914, 434 pp.
7. Breed, David R. *Preparing to Preach.* New York: George H. Doran Co., 1911, 455 pp.
8. Broadus, John A. *On the Preparation and Delivery of Sermons.* New York: Harper & Brothers, 1944.
9. Burrel, David J. *The Sermon: Its Construction and Delivery.* New York: Fleming H. Revell, 1913, 329 pp.
10. Byington, Edwin H. *Open-Air Preaching.* Hartford, Conn.: Hartford Theological Seminary, 1892, 104 pp. (inc. index).
11. Caemmerer, Richard R. *Preaching for the Church.* St. Louis: Concordia Publishing House, 1959, 353 pp. (inc. index).
12. Caldwell, Frank H. *Preaching Angles: Techniques and Procedures.* New York: Abingdon Press, 1954, 126 pp. (inc. index).
13. Cleland, James T. *Preaching to be Understood.* New York: Abingdon Press, 1965, 126 pp.
14. Coffin, Henry S. *What to Preach.* New York: George H. Doran Co., 1926.
15. Dabney, Robert L. *Sacred Rhetoric: Lectures on Preaching.* New York: Anson D. P. Randolph and Company, 1870, 361 pp.
16. Davis, Henry G. *Design for Preaching.* Philadelphia: Muhlenberg Press, 1958.
17. Davis, Ozora S. *Using the Bible in Public Address.* New York: Association Press, 1916, 184 pp.
18. Etter, John W. *The Preacher and His Sermon.* Dayton, Ohio: United Brethren Publishing House, 1891, 581 pp. (inc. index).

19. Evans, William. *How to Prepare Sermons and Gospel Addresses.* Chicago: Moody Press, n.d., 178 pp.
20. Ferris, Theodore P. *Go Tell The People.* New York: Charles Scribner's Sons, 1951, 116 pp.
21. Fisk, Franklin W. *Manual of Preaching: Lectures on Homiletics.* New York: A. C. Armstrong and Son, 1893, 337 pp. (inc. index).
22. Fritz, John H. C. *Essentials of Preaching: A Refresher Course in Homiletics for Pastors.* St. Louis: Concordia Publishing Co., 1948.
23. Fry, Jacob. *Elementary Homiletics: or, Rules and Principles in the Preparation and Preaching of Sermons.* Reading, Pa.: Henry H. Bieber, Printer, 1893, 57 pp.
24. Gibbs, Alfred P. *The Preacher and His Preaching.* Fort Dodge, Iowa: Walterick Printing Co., n.d.
25. Gibson, George M. *Planned Preaching.* Philadelphia: Westminister Press, 1954, 140 pp.
26. Graves, Henry C. *Lectures on Homiletics.* Philadelphia: American Baptist Publication Society, 1906, 156 pp.
27. Hogg, Wilson T. *A Handbook of Homiletics and Pastoral Theology.* Chicago: Free Methodist Publishing House, 1910, 454 pp. (inc. index).
28. Hogue, Wilson T. *A Handbook of Homiletics and Pastoral Theology.* Winona Lake, Indiana: Free Methodist Publishing House, 1949, 454 pp. (inc. index).
29. Hoppin, James M. *Homiletics.* New York: Dodd, Mead and Co., 1881, 809 pp.
30. _____. *The Office and Work of the Christian Minister.* New York: Sheldon and Co., 1869, 620 pp.
31. Hoyt, Arthur S. *The Preacher: His Person, Message and Method: A Book for the Classroom and Study.* New York: Macmillan Co., 1909, 380 pp.
32. _____. *The Work of Preaching: A Book for the Classroom and Study.* New York: Macmillan Co., 1905, 355 pp.
33. Jefferson, Charles E. *The Minister as Prophet. The Minister as a Shepherd.* New York: Thomas Y. Crowell & Co., 1905, 1912.
34. Johnson, Herrick. *The Ideal Ministry.* New York: Fleming H. Revell Co., 1908, 500 pp.
35. Jones, Ilion T. *Principles and Practice of Preaching.* New York: Abingdon Press, 1966, 272 pp. (inc. index and bibliography).
36. Jordan, G. Ray. *You Can Preach.* New York: Fleming H. Revell, 1951, 252 pp.

37. Kemp, Charles E. *Life Situation Preaching.* St. Louis: Bethany Press, 1956.
38. Kern, John Adam. *The Ministry to the Congregation: Lectures on Homiletics.* New York: Jennings and Graham, 1897, 551 pp.
39. Kidder, Daniel P., D.D. *A Treatise on Homiletics Designed to Illustrate the True Theory and Practice of Preaching the Gospel.* New York: The Methodist Book Concern, 1864, 504 pp.
40. Koller, Charles W. *Expository Preaching Without Notes plus Sermons Preached Without Notes.* Grand Rapids, Michigan: Baker Book House, 1969, 145 pp.
41. Linn, Edmund H. *Preaching as Counseling.* Valley Forge: Judson Press, 1966, 159 pp.
42. Littorin, Frank T. *How to Preach the Word with Variety.* Grand Rapids, Michigan: Baker Book House, 1953, 157 pp.
43. Luccock, Halford E. *In the Minister's Workshop.* Nashville, Tennessee: Abingdon-Cokesbury, 1944, 254 pp.
44. McBurney, James H. and Hance. *Discussion in Human Affairs.* New York: Harper & Brothers, 1950, 432 pp. (inc. index).
45. McComb, Samuel, D.D. *Preaching in Theory and Practice.* New York: Oxford Press, 1926, 231 pp.
46. McCracken, Robert J. *The Making of the Sermon.* New York: Harper & Brothers, 1956, 104 pp. (inc. index).
47. MacLennan, David A. *Pastoral Preaching.* Philadelphia: Westminster Press, 1955, 157 pp.
48. Mark, Harry C. *Patterns for Preaching.* Grand Rapids, Michigan: Zondervan Publishing House, 1959, 183 pp.
49. Monroe, Alan. *Principles and Types of Speech.* New York: Scott, Foresman & Co., 1939, 531 pp.
50. Montgomery, Richard A. *Preparing Preachers to Preach.* Grand Rapids, Michigan: Zondervan Publishing House, 1939, 249 pp.
51. Moore, William T. *Preacher Problems: or, Twentieth-Century Preacher.* New York: Fleming H. Revell Co., 1907, 387 pp.
52. Oates, Wayne E. *The Christian Pastor.* Philadelphia: Westminster Press, 1951, 171 pp.
53. Pattison, T. Harwood. *The Making of the Sermon.* Philadelphia: The American Baptist Publication Society, 1941, 391 pp. (inc. index).
54. Patton, Carl S. *The Preparation and Delivery of Sermons.* New York: Willett, Clark and Co., 1938, 191 pp.
55. Perry, Lloyd M. and Robert D. Culver. *How to Search the Scriptures.* Grand Rapids, Michigan: Baker Book House, 1967, 276 pp.

56. Perry, Lloyd M. *Manual for Biblical Preaching*. Grand Rapids, Michigan: Baker Book House, 1965, 215 pp.
57. Phelps, Austin. *The Theory of Preaching: Lectures on Homiletics*. New York: Charles Scribner's Sons, 1894.
58. Porter, Ebenezer. *Lectures on Homiletics and Preaching and on Public Prayer*. New York: Flagg, Gould and Newman, 1834, 428 pp.
59. Ray, Jefferson D. *Expository Preaching*. Grand Rapids, Michigan: Zondervan Publishing House, 1940, 123 pp.
60. Riley, William B. *The Preacher and His Preaching*. Wheaton, Illinois: Sword of the Lord Publishers, 1948, 146 pp.
61. Ripley, Henry J. *Sacred Rhetoric: or, Composition of Sermons*. Boston: Gould, Kendall and Lincoln, 1849, 259 pp.
62. Robbins, Howard C. *Preaching the Gospel*. New York: Harper & Brothers, 1939, 151 pp.
63. Sangster, W. E. *The Craft of the Sermon*. Philadelphia: Westminster Press, 1951, 208 pp. (inc. index).
64. Shedd, William G. T. *Homiletics and Pastoral Theology*. New York: Charles Scribner's Sons, 1895, 445 pp.
65. Skinner, Thomas H. *Aids to Revealing and Hearing*. New York: J. S. Taylor, 1839, 305 pp.
66. Sollitt, Kenneth W. *Preaching from Pictures*. Boston: W. A. Wilde, 1953, 150 pp.
67. Stidger, William L. *Building Sermons with Symphonic Themes*. New York: George H. Doran Co., 1926, 273 pp.
68. _____. *Preaching Out of the Overflow*. Nashville, Tennessee: Cokesbury Press, 1929, 238 pp.
69. Weatherspoon, Jesse B. *Sent Forth to Preach*. New York: Harper & Brothers, 1954, 183 pp.
70. Whitesell, Faris D. *The Art of Biblical Preaching*. Grand Rapids, Michigan: Zondervan Publishing House, 1950, 160 pp.
71. Whitesell, Faris D. and Lloyd M. Perry. *Variety in Your Preaching*. Westwood, New Jersey: Fleming H. Revell Co., 1954.
72. Wood, John. *The Preacher's Workshop: Preparation for Expository Preaching*. Chicago: Inter-Varsity Press, 1965.

INDEX

Adverbial Sermon 63
Amplification 35
Analogical Pattern 23, 43
Analogy 42, 43
Analytical Pattern 23, 49, 50, 58
Analytical Sermon 63
Apologetic Sermon 85–86
Approach Sentence 36
Argumentative Sermon 86
Astronomy Sermon 82
Audience 9, 113
Autobiographical Sermon 112

Believing Audience 9, 115
Bifocal Preaching 51
Book of the Bible Sermon 79

Categories of Thought 35
Categorizing Sermon 86
Chapter of the Bible Sermon 79
Chase Technique Sermon 51, 63
Christian Classic Sermon 81, 82
Church History Sermon 81, 82
Clarification Process 27, 42–51
Classification Sermon 86
Combinational Sermon 79–80
Commentary Sermon 86
Comprehensive Sermon 67
Conclusion 38–39, 43, 92–93
Content (Analysis) 20
Context (Surveying) 19
Corrective Sermon 86
Counseling Preaching 52
Couplet Sermon 63

Deductive Sermon 64–65
Definition 35, 36
Denominational Sermon 81, 82 83
Devotional Sermon 63
Dewey, John 52

Diagramming Ideas 21
Dialogue 120–121
Discussion in Human Affairs 52
Doctrinal Sermon 86–87
Doctrine 45–46
Doubtful Audience 9, 116–118
Dramatic Book Sermon 81, 83
Dramatic Continuity Sermon 64
Dramatic Sermon 112, 115

Ethical Preaching 52
Ethical Sermon 87
Etymological Pattern 23, 44–45
Evangelistic Sermon 87
Expansive Sermon 88
Experiential Sermon 88
Explanation (Sermonic) 37
Exposition 35
Expository Sermon 88

Facet Sermon 48, 64
Factual Data 19
Figures of Speech 21, 34
Foundational Pattern 23

Great Life Sermon 81, 82, 83
Great Painting Sermon 81, 82, 84
Great Poem Sermon 81, 82
Guessing Game Sermon 63

Hegelian Sermon 64
Hobby Sermon 82, 84
Homiletical Development 19
Homiletical Mind 18
Hostile Audience 9, 118–120
Hymn Sermon 81, 82

Illustrated Sermon 113
Illustrational Pattern 23, 46–48
Illustrations 55, 93–94

Imaginary Conversation Sermon 112
Implicational Pattern 23
Implicational Sermon 64–65
Inductive Sermon 64
Inferential Sermon 48–49, 64–65
Interrogation 36
Interrogative Adverbs 27–29, 33
Interrogative Pronouns 42
Interrogative Sermon 63
Interrogative Substitute 33
Introduction 36–38, 43, 91–92
Invention 9
Investigation Process 23, 51–55
Investigation Sermon Outline 54–55

Jewel Sermon 48, 64

Key Phrases 27–28, 33
Key Phrase Sermon 80
Key Words 22, 27, 33, 43
Key Word Sermon 80

Ladder Sermon 65
Life Situation Preaching 51
Life Situation Sermon 88
Logical Relationships 39

Main Point 35, 43, 81
Main Divisions 34–35, 91
Manual for Biblical Preaching 23
Memorizing 111
Messages from Notes 111
Microscopic Sermon 67
Modern Parable Sermon 82, 83
Modification Outline Check 56–58
Modification Process 23, 27–42, 81
Modification Sermon Outline 41–42, 58–60
Music Sermon 81, 82, 83–84

Narration 36
Narrative Sermon 89
Natural Sermon 67

Objections Answered Sermon 65
Objective Sentence 38
Object Sermon 82, 84
Observational Sermon 88
Oratorical Sermon 65
Orientation Sermon 89

Paragraph of the Bible Sermon 79–80
Pastoral Preaching 51
Personal Problem Preaching 51
Persuasive Sermon 89
Pictorial Sermon 43–44, 49–50, 65
Pilgrimage Sermon 65
Practical Sermon 46–48, 65
Preaching Portion
   Analyzing 20–21
   Selecting 17–18
   Studying 19–23, 29–43
Preparation
   General 11, 15–17
   Specific 17–23
Presentation of the Sermon 97–121
Preventative Preaching 52
Problematical Pattern 23
Problem Solving Preaching 51
Problems (Types of) 51
Proposition 32–34, 90
Propositional Sermon 65
Proposition (Types of) 32–34
Pyramid Sermon 65

Question Sermon 66
Quotation Sermon 82, 85

Rebuttal Sermon 86
Rhetorical Bridge 32–34
Roman Candle Sermon 45–46, 66

Scriptural Foundations 34, 40
Section Sermon 79–80
Selective Sermon 89
Sermon Processes 1, 27–55
Sermon Ideas (Search for)
   21–22
Sermon Items (Clarification
   Type) 43–51
Skyrocket Sermon 66
Slogan Sermon 82, 85
Social Preaching 52
Social Sermon 89
Soul Winning Sermon 87
Special Days and Seasons 97–107
Special Occasions 107–111
Spiritual Concept 43
Spiritualizing Sermon 89
Style 55–60
Subdivisions 35–36
Subpoints 43
Subject 29–32
Subject Survey 30
Suppositional Sermon 45–46, 66

Surprise Package Sermon 66
Symphonic Sermon 66
Synthetical Sermon 67

Telescopic Sermon 65
Testimony Sermon 82, 85
Textual Sermon 67
Thematic Sermon 89
Theme 30–32, 43
Theme Probing 31–32
Theological Sermon 86–87
Therapeutic Preaching 52
Three Point Sermon 64
Timeless Truth 32
Title 55, 56
Topical Sermon 89
Transitional Sentence 32–34, 43,
   81
Twin Point Sermon 67

Verse of the Bible Sermon 80

Word Study Sermon 44–45